Surviving the French Revolution

Surviving the French Revolution

A Bridge across Time

Bette W. Oliver

LEXINGTON BOOKS
Lanham • Boulder • New York • Toronto • Plymouth, UK

Published by Lexington Books
A wholly owned subsidiary of The Rowman & Littlefield Publishing Group, Inc.
4501 Forbes Boulevard, Suite 200, Lanham, Maryland 20706
www.rowman.com

10 Thornbury Road, Plymouth PL6 7PP, United Kingdom

British Library Cataloguing in Publication Information Available

Library of Congress Cataloging-in-Publication Data
Oliver, Bette Wyn, date.
Surviving the French Revolution : a bridge across time / Bette Oliver.
pages cm.
Includes bibliographical references and index.
ISBN 978-0-7391-7441-8 (cloth : alk. paper) — ISBN 978-0-7391-7442-5 (electronic)
1. France—History—Revolution, 1789–1799—Social aspects. 2. France—History—Revolution, 1789–1799—Refugees. 3. France—History—Revolution, 1789–1799—Influence. I. Title.
DC158.8.O45 2013
944—dc23
2012051430

ISBN 978-1-4985-1089-9 (pbk : alk. paper)

♾™ The paper used in this publication meets the minimum requirements of American National Standard for Information Sciences Permanence of Paper for Printed Library Materials, ANSI/NISO Z39.48-1992.

Printed in the United States of America

Contents

Acknowledgments   vii

Introduction   1

1 Crossing the Bridge   5

2 From Monarchy to Republic   19

3 French Émigrés in the United States   35

4 Artists and Writers   51

5 Rule by Terror   67

6 Flight of the Fugitives   81

7 Those Who Survived   95

Conclusion   111

Bibliography   121

Index   127

About the Author   135

Acknowledgments

As an independent scholar, I have benefited greatly from discussions with my colleagues in French history. The annual meetings of the Consortium on the Revolutionary Era 1750–1850 and the Western Society for French History have provided me with valuable opportunities to exchange ideas and consider useful suggestions about my work. The friendship and comments extended by my colleagues are all greatly appreciated.

Thanks are due also to the helpful staffs of the Bibliothèque Nationale-Richelieu, the Bibliothèque Doucet, and the Archives Nationales in Paris, where most of the research for this book took place.

I am grateful to Terry Sherrell of OneTouchPoint/Ginny's in Austin for her assistance and expertise in dealing with the electronic aspects of this book; to Professor Hermina Anghelescu of Wayne State University for compiling the index; and to Ann Seago and Maria Gonzalez for expediting book orders from the University of Texas Library.

Introduction

While historians of France tend to date events as having occurred either before or after the great revolution of 1789, those who were actually involved did not enjoy the benefit of such a measured perspective. For them the continuity of time had, in effect, been broken by the revolution. Events outpaced the days almost as if the normal sequence of minutes, hours, days, and weeks had been telescoped, and those who were caught up in the whirlwind had no idea of what to expect from one day to the next. The uncertainty and insecurity unleashed by the revolution created an atmosphere in which its participants had insufficient time to make judicious decisions. They were living in unknown territory after the fall of the Bastille in July 1789, with no precedents to follow and no directions to guide them, disconnected from the familiarity of the past and "stranded in the present."[1] While the leaders of the revolution were eager to achieve a better and more equitable form of government, others were nostalgic for the certainties of the Ancien Régime. Under the circumstances, these witnesses to history, much as in today's world, had little choice but to devise survival strategies according to their personal beliefs and goals, and hope that they had chosen wisely.

No one living in the early days of the revolution, however, could have foreseen its terrible end a few years later, least of all its leaders, who had entertained almost utopian visions of a moral regeneration in France. Elated by the recent success of the American Revolution, some were persuaded that France might be able to emulate that example. Unlike the United States, however, France was emerging from one thousand years of monarchical rule and a rigid social hierarchy, and those responsible for maintaining the institutions of the Ancien Régime were not enthusiastic proponents of the new order. The revolutionary leaders acknowledged as much and realized that they faced many difficulties, but they little imagined that it would take almost one hundred years for a successful French republic to emerge.

The instability of the period between 1789 and 1795 caused a number of persons to leave the country as soon as possible, while others remained until they were threatened with imprisonment or worse. Not surprisingly, some members of the royal family and many aristocrats feared (correctly, as it turned out) that if they did not leave quickly, they would not be allowed to leave at all. Most of these left France thinking that their exile would be brief and temporary, and they planned to return as soon as it was safe to do so. Others, however, left France with the intention of remaining elsewhere; they simply wanted nothing to do with the new government, which had in some cases eliminated their means of employment. These included members of the bourgeoisie, priests, artisans, domestic servants, laborers, and even a few aristocrats, who hoped to create a sort of paternalistic rural settlement in the New World. Although they were in no danger at that time, in 1790 a group of approximately one thousand dissatisfied men and women sailed to the United States to seek better opportunities on the Ohio frontier. Other French aristocrats, who planned on only a temporary exile, gravitated toward cities in the northeastern United States, especially Philadelphia.

Between 1789 and 1791, the revolutionary leaders worked together to try to accommodate Louis XVI, establishing what they hoped would be a workable constitutional monarchy. The king's aborted flight to Varennes in the summer of 1791, however, altered the course of the revolution, while his subsequent trial and execution resulted in irreconcilable divisions within the national assembly. Those Jacobin and Girondin deputies who formerly had worked together became bitter enemies, which led in the spring of 1793 to the expulsion of a group of Girondin legislators. Those deputies certainly had never imagined that they would be forced to flee from the very government that they had helped to create, but suddenly they were forced to decide which survival strategy to follow. Consequently, those who chose to remain in Paris were imprisoned and later executed, while those who fled managed to survive for a time as fugitives.[2]

The acceleration of time and the inability to predict what might happen next made it extremely difficult to choose the best course of action. In addition, the lack of reliable information coupled with the profusion of rumors and the delays in communication between Paris and the provinces only exacerbated the decision-making process. Most information was relayed orally, or in letters or newspapers, which reflected the biases of their editors. All too often, revolutionary events outpaced all available forms of communication, resulting not only in misunderstandings and confusion but also in real danger for those concerned.

Thus, it was not possible to grasp the full import of the period between 1789 and 1795 until time had decelerated to a more reasonable level sometime after the fall of Robespierre in July 1794. Even then, much that had transpired during those chaotic years remained hidden, often because the government that followed did not want to reveal incriminating details. The years between 1789 and 1795 produced a sharp division in the history of France. Those who had lived through that history said as much in their memoirs, many of which reflected a keen sense of loss and disillusionment. Time had been "broken" definitively in their lives; those who survived had effectively crossed a bridge between the Ancien Régime and the beginning of the modern world.

Drawing on the firsthand accounts of those involved—correspondence, memoirs, diaries, government reports, official documents, and newspapers—as well as later, more reflective treatments, this book examines how various representatives of French society chose to conduct their lives following the sudden changes ushered in by the revolution. The book focuses on several specific groups: those who fled from France as soon as possible after the fall of the Bastille, both those who planned to return and those who did not; those who remained and tried to take advantage of new opportunities; and those involved in the actual governing of France between 1789 and 1795.

The first group, mostly aristocrats and members of the royal family, also included a celebrated artist, Elisabeth Vigée-LeBrun, Marie Antoinette's portraitist and an avowed monarchist. Although she expected to be gone for a matter of months, her exile turned into twelve years, during which time (as documented in chapter 2) she traveled to the various courts of Europe, earning commissions on her paintings. The first group of exiles also includes those who left early in the revolution with no intention of returning, such as the émigrés who chose to settle in the Ohio wilderness in 1790. Others who chose temporary exile in the United States later in 1793 and 1794 included some prominent Frenchmen, among them Talleyrand, Madame de la Tour du Pin, and Moreau St. Méry. Their experiences are described in chapter 3.

Among those who remained in France, enhancing their careers in the process, were Vigée-LeBrun's husband, the art dealer Jean-Baptiste Pierre LeBrun, who managed to gain a position at the new national museum, thanks to the influence of the artist and ardent endorser of the revolution, Jacques-Louis David. In addition to LeBrun and David, the careers of the artists Adélaide Labille-Guiard, Anne Vallayer-Coster, and Marguerite Gérard, as well as those of the writers Sébastien Chamfort and André Chénier, are examined in chapter 4.

Several revolutionary leaders and their associates—Jacques-Pierre Brissot, François Buzot, Jean and Manon Roland, Jérôme Pétion, Maximilien Robespierre, Jacques Danton, and Honoré Riouffe—comprise the third group to be addressed. Their actions and survival strategies are covered in chapters 5, 6, and 7.

For the persons chronicled in this book, perceptions mattered decisively, even if they were mistaken, and timing was key to their survival. For example, if Louis XVI and his family had attempted to escape from Paris earlier in the revolution rather than in June 1791, they very well may have succeeded, thus changing the course of the revolution. In a similar vein, if the Girondin fugitives had chosen, while they were hiding in Brittany, to sail for England rather than taking their chances in the Bordeaux area, they quite possibly could have saved their lives. And if Robespierre and his associates had met defeat before the summer of 1794, thousands of prisoners would have been spared. As mentioned earlier, the rapid pace of unprecedented events and the distortions in communication played a vital role in the decision-making process of the participants in the revolution.

The judicious use of primary sources makes it possible to better understand the actions taken by those who are the focus of this book. While some of them realized too late that they might not have made the best choices for their survival, they faced adversity with not a little courage and steadfastness. Many of them also managed to leave behind invaluable written records of their thoughts and actions, some composed while they were in prison awaiting execution. Regardless of whether they survived and flourished or became victims of the guillotine, these memoirists did care what future generations might think about them and they went to great lengths to safeguard their writings. Their memoirs do not pretend to be objective, of course, since the authors meant to present themselves in the best light possible, while portraying their adversaries in a negative fashion.

In addition to using primary sources available in the Bibliothèque Nationale, the Bibliothèque Doucet, the Archives Nationales, and some departmental archives, as well as the Cincinnati Historical Society Library, references to relevant secondary sources are included to present a more comprehensive treatment of the period between 1789 and 1795.

NOTES

1. Peter Fritzsche, *Stranded in the Present: Modern Time and the Melancholy of History* (Cambridge, Mass.: Harvard University Press, 2004).

2. Bette W. Oliver, *Orphans on the Earth: Girondin Fugitives from the Terror, 1793–1794* (Lanham, Md.: Lexington Books, 2009).

ONE

Crossing the Bridge

Between the death of Louis XIV in 1715 and the beginning of the French Revolution in 1789, French society experienced a cultural transformation that manifested itself on a number of intersecting levels. It was a period of rising expectations, innovations and reforms, increasing literacy, and the exchange of ideas, with a growing sense of participation in a wider world open to trade and exploration. Despite the tendency of some earlier historians to view the Enlightenment as a period leading up to and culminating in the great revolution of 1789, it is doubtful that those alive at the time expected any such disruption. On the contrary, most eighteenth-century French citizens looked forward to a brighter and more comfortable future.

Paris, a capital city of approximately seven hundred thousand in 1780, served as a cultural and economic magnet drawing people from all over France and Europe. Tourists, government representatives, men of letters, students, and seasonal laborers came and went in the French capital, adding to its vitality and mobility. Although the king and court resided at Versailles, Paris was also the seat of power, home to the Parlement, the Académie, and the commercial center. In addition, according to historian Daniel Roche, "Parisians controlled a significant portion of France's wealth," a fact that increasingly would contribute to conflicts with provincial citizens, who frequently resented the power emanating from the capital.[1]

The rising expectations of French citizens had resulted from a period of prosperity and population growth prior to 1778. Between 1715 and 1789, the French population increased from eighteen million to twenty-six million, the largest in Europe at that time, although other European countries also experienced population growth during this period. France, however, unlike Britain, was slow to industrialize, which led to increased

unemployment, especially in the cities. Nevertheless, despite some work-
er unrest and the loss of some important overseas colonies, France appeared to be a strong country in the 1780s. Louis XVI could still be considered the father of his people, for the most part, even if his Austrian
queen was heartily disliked by many. Even the city of Paris appeared to
be under control, "the best-managed and best-policed city in Europe,"
with a comparatively low rate of violent crime.[2]

France, then, appeared to be secure in the 1780s. By aiding the colonists in the American Revolution, it had also gained in stature, while at
the same time dealing a blow to the British, its traditional enemy. The
French fascination with the New World, and specifically with North
America, had only increased since Benjamin Franklin's visits to Paris in
1767 and 1778. Yet even before that time, Voltaire's *Lettres philosophiques*
and Rousseau's evocations of the "noble savage" had contributed to the
American mystique, and even earlier, William Penn's charter for establishing Pennsylvania, granted by the English king in 1681, had been
translated and published in France, where the notions of religious toler-
ance, political freedom, and representative government found fertile
ground. Following the Treaty of Paris in 1763, the British territory in
North America had increased substantially, but the decisive defeat of the
French did not discourage their interest in North America.

The exchanges and correspondence between France and the American
colonies continued to develop during the 1760s and 1770s, including
foreign memberships in the French Royal Academy of Science, the
American Philosophical Society, and Masonic lodges. Franklin's influence in forging closer French-American connections not only served to
spread ideas of liberty and equality in France but also managed to annoy
the British government, which was trying to govern its colonies from
afar. French newspapers reported on the frictions between Britain and
her American colonies, which culminated in the Stamp Act of 1769. As a
result, literate Frenchmen were aware of the issues involved, and those
favoring reforms were inspired by the idealism shown by the American
leaders. Therefore, the American Revolution begun in 1776 precipitated a
series of changes that would, in turn, accelerate changes in the French
state as well.

French reformers, eager to follow the American example, ignored or
overlooked the very real differences between the American colonies and
France, namely history, geography, and political systems. Between 1776
and 1789, these reformers sought to make "Americanism" acceptable, not
only among enlightened intellectuals but also among the general populace. Americanists such as Jacques-Pierre Brissot de Warville described
the United States as "a union of democracies founded on the principle
that all power emanates from the people."[3] The translations and publications of the various state constitutions, the states' bills of rights, and the
Declaration of Independence had only served to increase the French lib-

erals' desires for change. Yet unlike the colonists, they lacked the experience of representative government and thus had no foundation on which to build a new French nation.

Since 1776, French visitors to North America, including those who had fought in the American Revolution, had contributed their firsthand reports about their adventures. Hector St. John de Crèvecoeur's *Lettres d'un cultivateur Americain* (1784), the most popular book about America, served to romanticize rustic life and natural beauty, much as had Rousseau. Crèvecoeur had journeyed to America at the age of nineteen, become a farmer, and married an American woman. His *Lettres* were translated and published in English in 1782. In 1787 he joined the writer Jacques-Pierre Brissot de Warville, the financier Etienne Clavière, and the lawyer Nicolas Bergasse to form the *Société Gallo-Américaine*, an organization to foster increased French-American trade.[4]

The more than nine thousand Frenchmen who had fought in the American Revolution came home with firsthand accounts of American ideals in action. While not all of them entertained high opinions of Americans in general, many of the early leaders of the French Revolution had been inspired by the American example. These included the Marquis de Lafayette, the Count de Rochambeau, Alexandre de Lameth, the Count de Ségur, and the Viscount de Noailles.[5] Some of these men were monarchists, but in 1789 the idea of a constitutional monarchy seemed eminently possible.

The transition from the absolute monarchy of the Ancien Régime to a constitutional one, however, would prove to be inherently difficult and cumbersome due to, among other things, the hierarchical social and political system. Rights and privileges were enjoyed by the clergy or First Estate (.05 percent of the population) and the nobility or Second Estate (1.5 percent of the population). The remainder of the population (about 98 percent) belonged to the Third Estate. The church's annual income, derived from land ownership, amounted to about half that of the royal government, and it was not taxed. While the nobility comprised only about 350,000 members, it benefited greatly from a near monopoly on royal administrative offices, the judiciary, and officers' commissions in the army, and was not subject to taxes. In addition, should a member of the nobility become involved in any sort of criminal activity, he could expect lenient treatment. As for the Third Estate, or the majority of Frenchmen, approximately 500,000 could be counted as members of the bourgeoisie; city workers amounted to 2,500,000; and the peasants or farmers numbered 22,500,000 (87 percent of the population). The diverse Third Estate included rich financiers (untaxed), as well as lawyers and merchants, shopkeepers, artisans, and industrial workers (all taxed), and well-to-do landowners, renters, and sharecroppers. Although the peasants owned 54 percent of the land, they were subject to not only heavy taxes but also feudal dues.[6]

Under such an inequitable system during a period of rising expectations, it is not surprising that many members of the bourgeoisie felt frustrated and dissatisfied. While the financiers or wealthy merchants saw their business opportunities expand through loans to the government or colonial trade, others, including lawyers, men of letters, booksellers, printers, and craftsmen, found their ambitions blocked. Those bourgeois parents who had sacrificed for the education of their children were often disappointed, because the best positions were taken by members of the nobility. The generation that entered adulthood in the 1780s, men such as Brissot de Warville, Desmoulins, Sieyès, and Barnave found that birth trumped merit in almost every case.[7]

By 1788 the lack of social mobility and opportunities for a rapidly increasing population combined with a worsening economic situation had led to a financial crisis. Prices and unemployment increased and the harvests of 1788 and 1789 were disappointing; bread riots erupted as the populace became ever more restive. Financiers were reluctant to increase loans to the Crown, because the state's expenditures exceeded its income by 100,000,000 to 150,000,000 livres a year.[8] Louis XVI's generosity to the American colonies had exacerbated France's financial problems, despite his efforts to initiate some reform efforts through his Comptroller Generals from 1774 through 1788. While Louis XVI might have intended to reform the government, he had not really supported his ministers in their efforts to rein in the debt. In addition, the clergy and nobles were not eager to contribute more through taxation unless they could exercise greater power. Consequently, hoping for a solution to the financial crisis, in August 1788 the king announced that he would call a meeting of the Estates General (representatives of the three estates) in May 1789.

The king's announcement was greeted initially with approval by members of the Third Estate. Their attitude changed abruptly, however, when the Parlement of Paris ruled that the Estates General must be constituted as it had been in 1614, the date of its last meeting—that is, representatives of the clergy, nobility, and commons would sit separately and vote as estates on the issues.[9] The members of the Third Estate in 1788 had no intention of docilely obeying a rule that they considered outmoded at the very least. They realized that their interests would surely suffer under such a system, because the clergy and nobles would vote together as privileged orders. The Abbé Sieyès, a liberal priest and persuasive writer, suggested that the Third Estate should have twice as many representatives as the other two estates and that voting should be "by head" instead of "by order." In response, the king announced in December 1788 that the Third Estate would have six hundred votes, and the other two estates three hundred votes each. He did not specify, however, that all three orders would vote together, which would have given the Third Estate more power.

That the Third Estate was able to succeed in this doubling of their representatives can be attributed to the influence of members of the "patriot" party, which also included some members of the nobility such as Lafayette and Condorcet, and of the Parlement, including Adrien DuPort and Hérault de Séchelles, who worked with academicians and writers to publicize their objectives. These men had formed ties through various social and political organizations throughout France, and now they used their connections to effect change through pamphlets and petitions. At this point the methods used by the Third Estate were rather moderate, with the exception of the Abbé Sieyès's famous pamphlet titled "What Is the Third Estate?" In it he boldly stated that the nation could do without the privileged orders very well; in fact, France would be better as "a prosperous whole."

While none at this point had suggested overtly that the monarchy should be abolished, the reform-minded Frenchmen from throughout the country did provide ideas of what they hoped for in their *cahiers des doléances*, or bills of grievances and requests. The *cahier* from Evreux, for example, called for *concorde* among the three estates, abolition of the *lettres de cachet*, a constitution, frequent meetings of the Estates General and the reestablishment of the provincial estates, and laws for liberty of the press and to protect non-Catholics, as well as judicial reforms and reduced prices for salt and tobacco. With ninety-three articles, the *cahier général de l'ordre du Tiers état du bailliage d'Evreux* was considered liberal, and even radical, by some at the time.[10] All of these measures would have been compatible with a constitutional monarchy, however, which was what most of the elected representatives of the Estates General had in mind.

Deputies to the Estates General were elected from each of the constituencies in France. The three hundred representatives elected for the First Estate included only forty-six bishops, notably Talleyrand, while most were parish priests. Among the three hundred nobles elected, there were ninety liberals, such as Lafayette and Adrien Duport. Lawyers formed the majority of the 578 deputies and 70 alternates chosen to represent the Third Estate. No workers or peasants were included among the rural representatives, but eighty-one "landed proprietors" were chosen.[11] The election of so many involved in legal practice, who were skilled in expressing their ideas, would prove decisive once the meeting of the Estates General got under way.

Another factor that influenced events during the summer of 1789 was the "outpouring of voices" in the public sphere. Since the abolition of pre-publication censorship in 1788, newspapers, pamphlets, and handbills had proliferated. The atmosphere of the capital city had changed; it appeared that "everyone was talking," according to the Marquis de Ferrières.[12] Jacques-Pierre Brissot de Warville, the reform-minded writer who had just returned to Paris after six months in the United States, found that in his absence his compatriots had undergone a remarkable change. "I left them in slavery," he wrote, "and I find them free." While he rejoiced in their new energy, he also cautioned against moving too fast to achieve the public good. "The regeneration of the people must occur under a constitution," which would guarantee equal rights for all, he wrote, acknowledging that much work would be required to organize the Estates General, write a constitution, stabilize and consolidate the French debt, and reform abuses.[13]

For his part, Brissot, who was not elected as a deputy from Chartres but was chosen as the president of his Paris district, Filles-Saint-Thomas, contributed greatly to the "outpouring of voices" by launching a news-paper, the *Patriote Français*, in April 1789. Brissot believed that in a popu-lous nation like France, newspapers could serve to instruct the people, citing Thomas Paine's *Common Sense* as having been essential to the suc-cess of the American Revolution. An independent press was necessary to attack "the centuries of despotism," Brissot wrote, and he intended to make his paper an instrument of change.[14] The *Patriote Français* would become an influential voice in factional politics from 1790 to 1793.

Following an elaborate opening ceremony, the first regular session of the Estates General opened on 5 May 1789. Held in the Salle des Menus Plaisirs at Versailles, the twelve hundred or so deputies found that, de-spite the freedom to speak, it was difficult to be heard in the cavernous space. In addition, the presence of "ordinary people" gathered to observe the debates increased the cacophony.[15] Altogether, it was not an ideal situation. The optimism that had been generated over the past year gave way to disappointment as the lack of real leadership from the king be-came apparent. The deputies of the Third Estate became even more disil-lusioned when they discovered that the three estates were expected to meet and vote in separate rooms.

Galvanized by their leaders, including the Count de Mirabeau, the Abbé Sieyès, and Jean-Sylvain Bailly, the Third Estate refused to comply, insisting instead that all of the elected deputies meet together in a nation-al assembly. As a result, the meeting of the Estates General came to a standstill until 17 June. By that time some of the deputies from the First and Second Estates had joined those of the Third Estate, and they de-clared themselves the National Assembly of France. Consequently locked out of the Salle des Menus Plaisirs, the deputies met instead in an indoor tennis court nearby, where they pledged to meet until "the Constitution of the kingdom is established"—the historic Tennis Court Oath. Hence-forth the National Assembly would discuss writing a constitution for what most of the deputies expected to be a constitutional monarchy under Louis XVI. The king, for his part, had agreed on some matters, including equal taxation, liberty of the press, and the creation of provin-cial assemblies. He insisted, however, on retaining power over matters affecting the privileges of the clergy and the nobility; thus, the deputies of the Third Estate refused to adjourn on 24 June. Most of the remaining clergy decided to join them, as did forty-seven nobles the next day, led by the king's cousin (but not his ally), the Duc d'Orléans. Surprisingly, Louis XVI then ordered his "royal clergy and nobility" to join the other deputies, now sitting as the National Assembly.[16]

While it appeared that the king had given in to the demands of the Third Estate, apparently he had not. Between 22 June and 1 July, he ordered twenty thousand troops from provincial garrisons to proceed to Paris. Most of these men were Swiss and German mercenaries under the command of a Swiss general, Baron Besenval. It was essential for the royal government to maintain order in Paris, where the people already felt insecure. Yet the presence of the troops only caused alarm, as rumors abounded that the National Assembly was in danger and that the king might be spirited away. On 11 July Louis XVI chose to dismiss Jacques Necker, his popular finance minister, thereby increasing the tensions in Paris. People poured onto the streets and crowds gathered at the Palais Royal, the center of opposition to royal authority under the protection of the Duc d'Orléans. There they were treated to stirring orations such as that of Camille Desmoulins, who urged the people, "To arms! To arms!" and "Defend the National Assembly!"

Disorder and looting occurred on the night of 12 July and the following day, at which time the Parisian deputies met at the Hotel de Ville to form a militia. It was their intent to provide arms to responsible property owners to help restore order and counter the king's troops. By 13 July, however, Parisian mobs had destroyed most of the custom posts and invaded prisons searching for arms. They had also stolen hundreds of kegs and bottles of wine from the monastery of Saint-Lazare, an action that only intensified the disorder. In addition, by the morning of 14 July, a crowd numbering approximately eighty thousand had removed thirty thousand muskets from the Invalides.[17]

Whatever hopes there had been of maintaining stability quickly disappeared as the unrest in the city increased. Armed crowds moved toward the Bastille, a royal fortress built in the 1300s, which had been used as a prison since 1660. The crowd believed that, in addition to prisoners, they would also find a large cache of arms and supplies. By 1789, however, only seven prisoners remained, and the royal government had already made plans to demolish the ancient building. The Count de Launey, commander of the Bastille, had access to eighty-two soldiers unfit for regular duty and thirty Swiss mercenaries, but he had not received any orders to defend the prison. No match for the mass of angry men massed outside, late in the afternoon de Launey sent out a note asking for an honorable surrender and departure for himself and his forces. Having received no reply by 5:30, he decided to lower the drawbridge and leave, but instead of being allowed to depart in peace, he and his men were arrested as the crowd pushed its way into the Bastille.

As de Launey and his men were being taken to the Hotel de Ville, the scene turned violent. Some enraged citizens took matters into their own hands and killed three officers and three veterans. Then, on the steps of the Hotel de Ville, the hapless de Launey was attacked in a brutal manner: the mob hacked him to pieces, placed his head on a pike, and carried it aloft through the streets.[18]

The king's troops under Besenval had not come to the aid of de Launey, but Besenval had sent a message urging him not to give in to the demands of the crowd. The message had been intercepted instead, thus leaving de Launey alone to decide what course to follow.[19] His fateful decision to surrender thus had set in motion a series of events that no one in Paris could have imagined. The spectacle of severed heads on pikes would become a familiar sight in the days after the fall of the Bastille, a sight that sickened some and thrilled others.

Gouverneur Morris, an American visiting Paris on business in the summer of 1789, witnessed the spectacle of "the Head and Body of Mr. de Foulon. . . . The Head on a Pike, the Body dragged naked on the Earth." Foulon had been appointed to fill Necker's position on 11 July. Already unpopular with Parisians for suggesting in 1775 that if they were hungry, they could eat hay, Foulon became the victim of their repressed anger. After decapitating him, the crowd showed their disdain by stuffing his mouth with hay. Louis-Jean Bertier de Sauvigny, intendant of Paris, suffered the same treatment. Gouverneur Morris, disgusted by such actions, wrote in his diary, "Gracious God, what a people."[20] He was not optimistic about the chances for the National Assembly to succeed in creating a new government.

Thomas Jefferson, also in Paris as minister plenipotentiary to France since 1785, did not find the violence so appalling. In a letter of 25 July to Maria Cosway in London, he wrote that "the cutting off heads is become so much à la mode, that one is apt to feel of a morning whether their own is on their shoulders." Jefferson even believed that "the great crisis was over," since the Third Estate held the majority.[21] His early optimism was misplaced, however, as unfolding events would prove.

Notwithstanding the unsettling events in the summer of 1789, it was still a time of great expectations. Jean-Baptiste Louvet, a writer and future Girondin deputy to the National Convention, described in his memoirs the "mélange of patriotism and love" in Paris, and the audacious "newness" of it all. He was pleased when some of the "so-called people" applauded as they observed the tricolor that he wore on his hat. It was impossible to see at that time, he wrote, the "calomnies" to come, when the "bonheur of this class of people" would turn odious in the future. The moderate royalist M. Clermont-Tonnerre reported, "Everything is new to us. We are seeking to regenerate ourselves; we are having to invent words to express new ideas."[22]

The fall of the Bastille signaled a number of changes almost immediately. Not only did the king return the popular Necker to office, but on 16 July the king himself appeared in Paris at the Hotel de Ville, where he joined the recently elected mayor, Sylvain Bailly. In front of a wildly enthusiastic crowd, Louis XVI then put on the blue and red cockade of the Paris militia, which would in turn become the official National Guard under the command of the Marquis de Lafayette. Guardsmen throughout France, referred to as fédérés, subsequently formed a real national army in support of the National Assembly. The cockade soon would add white, the color of the Bourbons, to the red and blue of Paris, thus creating the tricolor, a visible symbol of the revolution.[23]

Municipal leaders throughout France feared the disorders in Paris would spread to other cities. Thus, following the events of 14 July, they had wasted no time in enacting safety measures. By 1 August, the inhabitants of Evreux had adopted rules for establishing a militia, "la garde bourgeoise," chosen officers, and organized the ranks in great detail. Oaths of allegiance were sworn by 2 August.[24]

The most surprising event that summer occurred on the night of 4 August. During an all-night session, the liberal members and aristocrats in the National Assembly moved decisively to abolish feudal rights, thus ending the inequities of privilege and property rights that had been an integral part of the Ancien Régime. This remarkable and idealistic action produced various reactions, ranging from euphoria to fear and insecurity. The Marquis de Ferrières wrote to his wife about the "memorable session," but he also advised her to stop all repairs on the chateau and to secure in a safe place all of the papers dealing with feudal obligations on their properties. Above all, he urged that she conserve cash, since no one knew what might happen next.[25]

François Buzot, a lawyer and deputy from Evreux, wrote to his constituents about the discussions on the rights of men and the night of 4 August, which filled him with "joy." He also assured them that he would send written reports of the proceedings, and he asked that a place be reserved for him in the "patriotic militia." Aware that some members of the nobility and clergy already regretted their hasty abandonment of ancient privileges, Buzot voiced strong support for those who had voted to abolish feudal rights, knowing that his opinion would not be welcomed by all of his constituents.[26] They would unleash their anger against him soon enough.

Buzot, like most of the deputies in the National Assembly during the early years of the revolution, took his duties seriously. As the representative of Evreux, he tried to keep his constituents informed about the proceedings in Paris through voluminous correspondence. He was not filled with radical ideas at that time, nor were most of the other deputies. Historian Timothy Tackett has written that, for the most part, "the deputies revealed themselves to be practical men, intense and passionate, yet pragmatic and capable of compromise."[27]

The idealism of 1789 would be eloquently expressed in the Declaration of the Rights of Man and the Citizen, the preface to the new constitution, which would be completed during the less idealistic days of 1791. The Declaration, passed by the National Assembly on 27 August, held that men were born and remained free and equal in rights. Furthermore, it stated that liberty, property, security, and resistance to oppression were "natural and inalienable rights." Equality before the law and freedom of speech and the press, as well as religious freedom, were promised, but voting qualifications were not mentioned. The king, disturbed by the extreme egalitarianism of such stated principles, allowed the document to be printed, but he refused to sign it. By September the king's veto power and the form of the future national legislature had become major issues that served to increase dissension among the various factions in the National Assembly.

The Patriot Party, comprised of the majority *constitutionnels* and the minority *monarchiens*, split over these two issues. The *constitutionnels*, led by Lafayette, Sieyès, and Barnave, favored no royal veto power and a unicameral legislature, while the *monarchiens*, led by Mounier, wanted absolute royal veto power and a bicameral legislature. The two factions finally compromised, settling on a unicameral body and a three-year suspensive veto, which Louis XVI found not at all to his liking. He saw it, in effect, as a blow to monarchical power, "abdicating divine right and divine duty to God." He reacted unwisely, as it turned out, by ordering a regiment of troops from Flanders to come to Versailles.[28]

The king had failed previously to consider the influence of public opinion, notably on 14 July, when the royal fortress had been invaded, and he chose to do nothing about it. Either he actually did not see it as a rebuff to royal authority or he preferred to ignore it. His indecisive nature did not serve him well in the summer and early autumn of 1789, when the public perceived royal authority as lessening by the day. What happened next during the so-called October Days would effectively signal that the power of the monarchy had been decisively eroded.

On 1 October, when the troops from Flanders arrived at Versailles, the king and queen presided over a banquet in honor of the officers. The ladies of the court dressed in white and wore lilies, both symbols of the Bourbon monarchy, and the officers replaced their tricolor cockades with white or black (Austrian) ones. News of this insult to the National Assembly reached Paris that very night, to be made public by journalists and orators the next day. The public wasted little time in reacting to news of the royal banquet. When the women of Paris, already angry about the high price of bread, went to their markets on 5 October, they discovered an acute shortage of bread, because the canals north of Paris were blocked by ice, which had prevented the transport of grain. Rather than return to their homes empty-handed, a crowd of some three thousand women marched to the Hotel de Ville and demanded bread. They settled for arms instead and appropriated food, horses, and wagons on their twelve-mile march to Versailles. The March of the Women, a visible representation of citizen unrest, became an event with major consequences for the monarchy.

The king did agree to receive a delegation of fifteen women and fifteen National Assembly deputies that evening, and he promised to order the release of grain supplies for Paris. For good measure, he notified the National Assembly that he would accept the Declaration and the veto measure. At that point, the situation appeared to be under control. Lafayette and the National Guard had arrived to oversee the crowd gathered outside, and the king's troops maintained watch inside the palace. The next morning, however, some men managed to slip inside, where they killed two royal guards near the queen's apartment. The interlopers were forced outside by the National Guard, but meanwhile the crowd had become restive, even parading one of the royal guard's heads on a pike. They also insisted that it was time for the king and queen to return with them to Paris, and Lafayette agreed that such a move might reassure the city's inhabitants. While Louis XVI and Marie Antoinette certainly would have preferred to remain in Versailles, they felt that they had little choice but to join the National Guards and the crowd, along with sixty members of the National Assembly, and depart for Paris. Once there, the royal family reluctantly took up residence in the Tuileries, a palace next to the Louvre. A few days later, the remaining deputies also moved to Paris and the National Assembly began holding their sessions in the Manège, an old riding school near the Tuileries.[29]

While the Parisians seemed pleased to have the royal family under their watchful eyes rather than in the palace at Versailles, the king soon enough would realize that he had become, in effect, a prisoner of Paris. His ancestor, Louis XIV, had chosen to live at Versailles because he understood how quickly the crowds in the capital could be moved to violence and he preferred not to be living among them in the palace of the Louvre. By agreeing to take the fateful step of moving to Paris, the king had placed himself, his family, and even to some extent the National Assembly in a position where they could be threatened or coerced by the citizens of Paris.

The "October Days," as they became known, added to the sense of euphoria and urgency that had enveloped the capital. Brissot wrote in the *Patriote Français*, "The events that have taken place right in front of us appear almost like a dream." He remarked upon "this astonishing Revolution" and his exhaustion caused by "guard service." Further on in his memoir he recalled his observation that "minutes are as centuries in revolutions."[30] More recently, the historian Lynn Hunt has stated, "A new relationship to time would turn out to be the single greatest innovation of the revolution."[31]

Contemporary accounts of the days following the fall of the Bastille provide evidence of the sense of acceleration experienced during this period. As the Marquis de Ferrières wrote in a letter of 17 July, "Events, my friend, succeed one another at such a pace that a single week fills the space of a year."[32] Coupled with this new sense of accelerated time was the inability to plan for even the near future. Rumors and delayed or unreliable communication only added to the overall feelings of uncertainty and anxiety, the sense of a lack of direction. If these sentiments were prevalent among those who championed the changes and reforms occurring in France and entertained great hopes that a constitutional monarchy could be realized, such feelings were greatly intensified in those who saw temporary exile as the safest course to follow.

NOTES

1. Daniel Roche, translation by Arthur Goldhammer, *France in the Enlightenment* (Cambridge, Mass./London: Harvard University Press, 1998), 645.

2. Owen Connelly, *French Revolution/Napoleonic Era* (New York: Holt, Rinehart and Winston, 1979), 10–13.

3. Durand Echeverria, *Mirage in the West: A History of the French Image of American Society to 1815* (New York: Octagon Books, Inc., 1966).

4. Robert Darnton, *George Washington's False Teeth: An Unconventional Guide to the Eighteenth Century* (New York: W. W. Norton, 2003), 123, 127.

5. Connelly, *French Revolution*, 31.

6. Connelly, *French Revolution*, 40–52.

7. Georges Lefebvre, translation by R. R. Palmer, *The Coming of the French Revolution* (Princeton, N.J.: Princeton University Press, 1947), 42–49.

8. Connelly, *French Revolution*, 59.

9. Connelly, *French Revolution*, 64.

10. Lefebvre, *Coming of the French Revolution*, 52, 61, 72; Connelly, *French Revolution*, 68; and Jacques Hérissay, *Un Girondin, François Buzot* (Paris: Perrin et Cie., Libraires-Editeurs, 1907), 28–29, 36.

11. Connelly, *French Revolution*, 67.

12. Sophia Rosenfeld, "AHR Forum on Being Heard: A Case for Paying Attention to the Historical Ear" (316–34), *American Historical Review* 116, no. 2 (April 2011), 327.

13. Cl. Perroud, ed., *J.-P. Brissot, Mémoires, 1754–1793* (Paris: Librairie Alphonse Picard & Fils, 1910), II: 191–94.

14. Perroud, ed., *J.-P. Brissot, Mémoires*, II: 179–183.

15. Rosenfeld, "On Being Heard," AHR (April 2011), 329–30.

16. Connelly, *French Revolution*, 69–73.

17. Connelly, *French Revolution*, 75, 78–80.

18. Connelly, *French Revolution*, 80–82.

19. Lefebvre, *Coming of the French Revolution*, 116.

20. Warren Roberts, "Gouverneur Morris and Thomas Jefferson: Two Americans in Paris in 1789" (31–40), *Consortium on the Revolutionary Era, 1750–1850 Selected Papers, 2008*, 31–32; William Howard Adams, *Gouverneur Morris: An Independent Life* (New Haven, Conn.: Yale University Press, 2003), 192–93.

21. Adams, *Gouverneur Morris*, 190.

22. Jean-Baptiste Louvet, *Mémoires de J. B. Louvet, l'un des Réprésentans Proscrits en 1793*, N. A. F. 1730, 140 (Paris: Bibliothèque Nationale, Dept. des Manuscrits); Caroline Moorehead, *Dancing to the Precipice: Lucie de la Tour du Pin and the French Revolution* (London: Chatto & Windus, 2009), 117.

23. Connelly, *French Revolution*, 82.

24. Hérissay, *Un Girondin*, 49–50.

25. Marquis de Ferrières, *Correspondance Inédité* (Paris: Armand Colin, 1932), 110–11. Quoted from a letter of 7 August in a paper presented by Alan Williams at the 2009 conference of the Western Society for French History in Boulder, Colorado.

26. Hérissay, *Un Girondin*, 51–53.

27. Timothy Tackett, *Becoming a Revolutionary: The Deputies of the French National Assembly and the Emergence of a Revolutionary Culture 1789–1790* (Princeton, N.J.: Princeton University Press, 1996), 312.

28. Connelly, *French Revolution*, 86–87.

29. Connelly, *French Revolution*, 87–90.

30. *Le Patriote Francais*, no. 63 (7 Octobre 1789): 3. Quoted by Lynn Hunt in her AHA Presidential Address, "The World We Have Gained: The Future of the French Revolution" (1–19), *The American Historical Review* 108, no. 1 (February 2003). See also Perroud, ed., *J.-P. Brissot, Mémoires*, II: 221–22.

31. Hunt, AHR (2003), 6.

32. Williams, WSFH paper, 3 (quoted from Marquis de Ferrières, *Correspondance Inédité*, 92).

TWO

From Monarchy to Republic

The first group of émigrés to seek safety outside of France included the king's younger brother, the Comte d'Artois, the future Charles X, who left in late July 1789. He would be followed by a growing number of fearful aristocrats, who expected their exiles to be temporary, perhaps only a matter of months, until the monarchy could regain control. By mid-1791 most royalists had emigrated, among them the king's other brother, the Comte de Provence, who would become Louis XVIII in 1814. Most of these early émigrés had settled in the German states, Switzerland, or England, near enough to return home in a relatively short time. Their presence outside of France would contribute to the conspiracy theories and threats of invasion that were prevalent from 1791 until 1793. Approximately 150,000 émigrés, mostly aristocrats, officers of the royal army, and higher ecclesiastics, would leave France between 1789 and the summer of 1794.[1]

The frontiers remained open until the king's flight to Varennes in June 1791, after which various measures were passed to regulate emigration, but the greatest number of émigrés would leave during the Terror in 1793 and 1794. The advent of war and the increasing radicalization of the revolution led to the emigration law of 8 April 1792 concerning the confiscation of property and the Act of 28 March–5 April 1793, which established a comprehensive emigration code.[2] After 25 October 1792, however, émigrés faced the death penalty if they returned; even so, a greater number of ordinary citizens chose to leave France than during the early years of the revolution, when the upper classes and nobility had felt the most threatened.[3] In addition, counter-revolutionary activities in the northwest and southeast regions of France led to higher percentages of emigration than from other areas of the country.[4] Consequently, émigré colonies developed in a number of European cities, including Turin,

Brussels, Coblenz, Worms, London, Lausanne, and Fribourg, and even in the United States, which became a haven for as many as ten thousand families.[5]

A majority of the émigrés found themselves in perilous financial and emotional circumstances. Believing that their exiles would be of a short duration, most had not foreseen the amount of time they would be away from home. Their lives had altered suddenly, causing them to lose not only property and possessions but important social connections as well. As the historian Peter Fritzsche has written about the revolutionary period, many émigrés found that they had become displaced physically and emotionally, cut off from the familiar world that they had known and "stranded in the present."[6]

Among those first voluntary émigrés who left France in the summer and fall of 1789 was the artist, Elisabeth Vigée-LeBrun, whose portraits of Marie Antoinette and various aristocrats had made her famous. Those portraits, seen by thousands at the Salon exhibitions, also had focused attention on her connections with the court, especially the 1787 portrait of "Marie Antoinette and her Children," referred to as "Madame Deficit" by critics of the queen. Vigée-LeBrun was one of only four women artists to have been accepted, in 1783, into the Académie Royale de Peinture et de Sculpture, a major achievement for a woman in the eighteenth century. After 1783 the Académie decided to limit the number of women artists to only four.[7] In addition, her Parisian home, the Hotel LeBrun, which she shared with her husband, the art dealer Jean-Baptiste Pierre LeBrun, and their daughter Julie, had become an easily identifiable target for malcontents who roamed the streets. Its edifice was distinctive, ornamented by a façade in the shape of a hemicycle. Designed by the architect Jean-Armand Raymond, the rather grand townhouse on the rue du Gros Chênet included an art gallery and a salesroom, which adjoined her husband's Hotel de Lubert on the rue de Cléry.[8]

Vigée-LeBrun wrote in her memoir about the fear she felt in 1789, when sulfur was thrown into the basement windows and "coarse sans-culottes" shook their fists at her when she stood near the windows.[9] Her fears increased to such an extent that she could no longer paint, while her artistic and social associations that once had been a source of great pride became political liabilities. She already had taken the precaution of obtaining passports for herself, Julie, and the governess; she was preparing to leave Paris in a public coach so as not to call attention to herself. On 6 October, the same day that her patron, the queen, would leave Versailles, Vigée-LeBrun left Paris. Dressed as a peasant woman with her face half-covered, because she was easily recognizable, the artist, along with her daughter and the governess, took her place in the public coach at midnight. Her brother Louis Vigée, her husband, and an old friend, the artist Hubert Robert, had escorted them as far as the usually turbulent Saint Antoine area. On the night of 6 October, however, its inhabitants apparently were fatigued due to their strenuous march from Versailles and were resting inside their homes. By the time that Vigée-LeBrun's coach passed, the streets were quiet.

Heading for the safety of Italy, Vigée-LeBrun carried with her only a few clothes and eighty louis; she planned to be away for only a year at most. She had left behind with her husband, in addition to paintings, jewels, and dresses, "the fruit of my labors," all of the money that she had earned as an artist. She recounted proudly in her memoir that, once out of France, she lived solely off of the proceeds received from her painting commissions, even managing to send money back to her husband to relieve his frequent financial distress.[10] The sight of new vistas had always lifted her spirits, and she described the scenery along the Echelles as "enchanting," which helped her to forget temporarily the troubles left behind in France.[11] She could not have imagined then that she would not be able to return for twelve long years.

Still, Vigée-LeBrun was more fortunate than many other émigrés, because her talent and reputation enabled her to travel throughout Europe seeking commissions for her work. A portrait by Vigée-LeBrun, one of France's most celebrated artists, served as a status symbol in eighteenth-century Europe. In addition to being a fine artist, she was also a lovely and interesting woman with good business sense, a great advantage in achieving financial security. She traveled extensively out of financial necessity, settling for varying periods of time wherever she found good sources of patronage. The vivid descriptions in her memoir of natural wonders, antiquities, and museums tend to overshadow the hard work that produced nearly two hundred portraits during her exile; she would return home with over one million francs for her efforts.

Many of the rulers in Western Europe were sympathetic to the Bourbon cause and welcomed Marie Antoinette's favorite portrait painter, along with the other émigrés that were filling their cities. She was warmly welcomed in Italy, where she gloried in the artistic treasures of Florence and was especially impressed by the collection of artists' self-portraits at the Uffizi. She would contribute her own self-portrait the next year in Rome, where it was exhibited to great acclaim.[12] Elected a member of the Roman Academia di San Luca in April 1790, Vigée-LeBrun remained in Rome, interrupted by several visits to Naples, until 1792. She enjoyed painting and socializing with other émigrés, but she reported that she avoided contact with the Polignac family, because she feared that such an association might cause problems for the Vigée and LeBrun families in Paris. Above all, she did not want to be accused of participation in some sort of Bourbon conspiracy.[13]

Before leaving Rome, Vigée-LeBrun painted the portraits of Louis XVI's aunts, Adélaide and Victoire, known as Mesdames Tantes, who had lived in Rome since 1791. The aunts had actually preferred the work of another artist, Adélaide Labille-Guiard, but since that artist had embraced the revolution, and Vigée-LeBrun was in Rome, they decided to sit for her.[14]

Vigée-LeBrun's short visits to Naples proved productive, resulting in a number of portraits, including that of the actress Emma Hart, who would become Lady Hamilton in 1791. She also received a commission to paint a portrait of the children of the Queen of Naples, Maria Carolina, a sister of Marie Antoinette who had married Ferdinand IV. She painted a portrait of the queen as well, finding her to be elegant and generous, although not as pretty as Marie Antoinette.[15] Her finest portrait in Naples was that of Italy's foremost operatic composer, Giovanni Paisiello; the portrait won critical acclaim when it was shown at the Paris Salon in 1791. It was even admired by the artist Jacques-Louis David, a champion of the revolution, who still managed to praise the fine work of a monarchist![16] It is one of the ironies of this period that David and J.-B.P. LeBrun were both working to establish the first national museum in France while Vigée-LeBrun was living as an émigrée and sending her work to the Salons.[17]

The artist left Italy for Vienna in the fall of 1792. She had hoped to be able to return to France, but the addition of her name to the list of émigrés had made such a move impossible. She would remain in Vienna for two and a half years, painting at least thirty-two portraits, including ten of Polish nobility and a number of pastels.[18] As in Italy, she enjoyed participating in Viennese society, which included at that time a number of émigrés including the Polignac family, the Duc de Richelieu, and her special friend and former patron, the Comte de Vaudreuil. He had left Paris at the same time as the Comte d'Artois, his friend and a major art collector like himself. Vaudreuil was a man variously described as "the eighteenth-century courtier par excellence" and "everything the revolutionaries had in mind when they characterized the court as a playpen of spoiled and greedy children."[19] Vigée-LeBrun, however, found that Vaudreuil possessed "all the qualities, all the charm, that make a man amiable," the kindest of men and a symbol of everything good. Tall and graceful, with "features as agile as his thoughts," and possessing a remarkable knowledge of painting, he appeared to be her ideal man. Not surprisingly, rumors indicated that Vaudreuil had been not only an important patron of Vigée-LeBrun's but also her lover.[20]

Vaudreuil's long friendship with the king's brother, the Comte d'Artois, had led to other important connections at court, notably to the queen's favorite, Yolande de Polignac, who became his mistress. Such a relationship provided a means to gain lucrative appointments for himself and his friends. His lavish lifestyle, however, often surpassed the income from his inherited Caribbean plantations; thus, he borrowed from the royal treasury to pay off his creditors. His influence had contributed to Vigée-LeBrun's position as an important court artist and had helped her husband attract many highly placed customers to his gallery. Vaudreuil also authorized LeBrun to furnish him with works of art and to organize sales for him.[21] It had been a profitable arrangement for all concerned, and Vigée-LeBrun defended Vaudreuil many years later in her memoir, noting how difficult it was to explain "the urbane charm, the easy grace, in short all those pleasing manners which, forty years ago were the delight of Parisian society." She greatly regretted the disappearance of the sort of gallantry associated with the Ancien Régime, affirming that "the women ruled then; the revolution has dethroned them."[22]

It is no surprise, therefore, that Vigée-LeBrun was delighted to see her old friend again in Vienna, a place she praised as exhibiting the same customs and tastes as found in Paris. Obviously pleased to be in Marie Antoinette's native land, Vigée-LeBrun romanticized descriptions of Vienna in her memoir, leading the reader to believe that even the peasants were happy under the benevolence of the Hapsburgs.[23]

She moved again in April 1795 for what she thought would be a short visit to Russia and the court of Catherine II. Arriving in Saint Petersburg in late July, after stops in Prague, Dresden, Berlin, and Riga, she rented an apartment near the Winter Palace. She wrote of being overwhelmed by the sights—the great monuments, fine public buildings, wide streets, the Neva River, and the architectural style and dress of the inhabitants, which reminded her of the time of Agamemnon.[24]

As in France, Italy, and Austria, Vigée-LeBrun was patronized and entertained by the royal family and nobility in Russia. She reportedly developed a real fondness for the country and its people, whom she found particularly hospitable toward persons of talent, and she would refer to Russia as her second home. She renewed contacts with the French émigrés in Saint Petersburg, which were so numerous, wrote the Prince de Ligne, "Madame LeBrun will soon think she is in Paris, there are so many French people at these gatherings."[25] The Comte d'Artois arrived in 1793 and was warmly welcomed by Catherine II, but apparently she did not find him to be as clever a politician as she had hoped. As leader of the émigrés, he sought help from other European governments to launch an offensive against the revolutionaries in France. He did receive from the empress a million rubles and a line of credit at the Russian embassy in London, but not the military aid that he had requested.[26]

During her six years in Russia Vigée-LeBrun pursued a busy work schedule, painting as many as sixty-seven portraits and earning as much as 121,400 rubles, or 402,000 francs. According to her memoir, she worked from dawn to dusk, Sundays excepted.[27] In addition, she even managed to send two paintings to the Salon of 1798 in Paris, the first ones she had sent since 1791, when three of her works had been exhibited.[28] It will be recalled that David had been highly complimentary of her 1791 portrait of Paisiello and considered her a fine artist, even if he did not agree with her politics. As an active member of the revolutionary government, he used his influence to help not only J.-B.P. LeBrun in his advisory capacity with the national museum but other artists as well.

Vigée-LeBrun's husband, ever short of funds, had sent her some "Old Master" paintings to sell in Russia. Although she explained in a letter that she had made every effort to sell them, she was not successful. Actually, LeBrun was fortunate that his "Old Masters" had not been destroyed in a fire that almost consumed the house, loaned to her by Countess Stroganoff, where his wife was staying in January 1801.[29] By this time Vigée-LeBrun was becoming anxious to leave Russia and return home. She felt the need for "rest, sunshine, and a warm climate," and suffered from depression due to a strained relationship with her daughter, who had made an unwise marriage, and the recent death of her mother in Paris. As she wrote to her son-in-law, "I would not wish to die in Moscow for the world."[30]

Fortunately for Vigée-LeBrun, she would not have to end her days in Russia. Her name had been removed from the list of émigrés on 5 June 1800, and she could return safely to France. After brief stops in Berlin, Dresden, Weimar, Gotha, and Frankfurt, Vigée-LeBrun crossed the border into France and arrived in Paris on 18 January 1802. Twelve years had passed since her departure, and she would find her native country greatly changed in her absence. "This France that I was re-entering had been the scene of the most atrocious crimes; but this same France was still my country," she wrote.[31] The loss of her mother and the many victims of the Revolution cast a pall over her return, and the revolutionary slogans scrawled on the public buildings reminded her of the executions of Marie Antoinette and Louis XVI. Had she not fled when she did, however, she did not doubt that she herself would have been among the victims.[32]

If Vigée-LeBrun had managed to survive the revolution by fleeing from France, her husband had pursued his own survival strategies in her absence. LeBrun's position in 1792 remained precarious, not only because he had acted as the keeper of pictures for both the Comte d'Artois and the Duc d'Orléans, but also because his wife had been the queen's portraitist and was among the first émigrés in 1789. A great deal had happened in the political arena since her departure. By 1790 the National Assembly had accelerated a number of reforms, which included abolishing religious orders as well as hereditary titles, dividing the country into eighty-three departments, and adopting the Civil Constitution of the Clergy, which held that bishops and priests were to be elected like other public officials. Then, in November 1790, the assembly had issued a decree requiring a loyalty oath from the clergy to the Civil Constitution, a move guaranteed to cause division within the religious establishment and among the populace.

By the spring of 1791, many of the deputies remained hopeful about the progress of the revolution. Louis XVI had sworn to uphold the constitution of 1791 in which his powers were defined and limited. With the consent of the Legislative Assembly, convened 1 October, the king could declare war and make peace and appoint ministers, ambassadors, and military officers; the ministers, however, were answerable to the Legislative Assembly. In addition the king was allowed a three-year suspensive veto. Composed of 745 deputies from 83 departments in France, plus some from the colonies, the new assembly was to be elected and to meet every two years, and the king did not have the power to dissolve it. Male citizens twenty-five years or older, who paid a "tax equal to the three days wages of a common laborer," were considered as "active citizens" and had the right to vote in the primary assemblies where electors were chosen; the electors, in turn, chose the deputies and the other officials.[33]

The deputy François Buzot, one of the leaders of the Brissotin faction in the National Convention, wrote in his memoir that it had been a mistake to leave Louis XVI on the throne: "The Constitution of 1791 had offered only that the two parties, the state and the prince, would be continually at war." He held (prophetically, as it turned out) that the Constitution "provided a state of necessary discord, which could finish only by the destruction of one or the other." In addition, the lack of safeguards in the Constitution of 1791 and the "lack of moderation" in the French people unfortunately worked against creating a republic like that in America, according to Buzot.[34]

Although Louis XVI had sworn to uphold the constitution, he had become increasingly unhappy and restless living in Paris surrounded by the revolutionary government and the unpredictable crowds. He had realized too late that he should have left the country in 1789, while it still might have been possible. By June 1791, he had finally agreed with Marie Antoinette and decided to follow the escape plan outlined by Count Axel Fersen of the Royal Swedish Regiment, who also was reported to be the queen's lover. Had the king adhered to that plan, it might have succeeded. The royal family, in disguise, managed to depart by coach on the night of 20 June, headed for Varennes, a town on the French border of the Austrian Netherlands in what is now Belgium. The unscheduled stops to rest or to eat along the route all but guaranteed that the finely detailed plan drawn up by Fersen would fail. Soon enough the king was recognized by a soldier, who reported the royal family's presence to authorities. By 25 June, accompanied by representatives of the national assembly and the National Guard, the royal family was once more escorted to Paris, where this time they truly would become prisoners of the revolutionary government.[35]

By July 1791, faced with the deception of the king, the deputies already had begun to discuss the possibility of forming a republic rather than a constitutional monarchy, while Parisians also had shown their displeasure by demonstrating and defacing symbols of royalty. Radical deputies held that the king should be judged for his betrayal, but the moderates opposed such an action. It was decided that until the constitution had been completed and the king had agreed to sign it, his executive powers were to be suspended. Should he refuse to accept and sign it, he would be deposed.[36]

By mid-1791 most of the ultra royalists as well as alarmed bankers and businessmen and "conservative constitutionalists" had emigrated. Many, including the king's brothers, had joined together in the Rhineland states, from where it was feared by the revolutionary government that they might gather forces for an invasion of France. On 31 October 1791, the Legislative Assembly ordered the Comte de Provence to return within two months or lose his rights to succession; he refused. At that point the assembly issued a decree ordering all émigrés to return to France by 1 January 1792, or face being legally classified as traitors and subject to punishment by death.[37] Although Louis XVI vetoed the decree, in December 1791 the Legislative Assembly forced him to order the Elector of Trier to expel the émigrés or be treated as an enemy. Leopold II complied with the order, but the German states continued their sympathetic treatment of the émigrés, while the Prince of Condé had managed to assemble an army of two thousand men in Worms.

In January 1792 the Legislative Assembly again coerced the king to sign an ultimatum to Leopold II demanding that he "renounce all anti-French treaties or face dire consequences." Leopold, however, was not intimidated and he refused; he also blamed the Jacobins for stirring up international tensions. Leopold died in March, to be succeeded by Francis II, his son and the nephew of Marie Antoinette. Also that March Louis XVI appointed a Girondin-led ministry that favored war.[38] The newspaper editor and Girondin deputy Jacques-Pierre Brissot (he had dropped "de Warville") urged taking the offensive against those foreign princes who had encouraged the émigrés, arguing that an open conflict would be preferable to an undeclared and prolonged one. The Jacobin leader Maximilien Robespierre's voice was one of the few reasonable ones raised against going to war at that time. He declared, "The thing for us to do is to set our own affairs in order and to acquire liberty for ourselves before offering it to others."[39] Brissot and Robespierre continued their arguments regarding the war at meetings of the Jacobin Club.

Under increasing pressure, the king appeared before the Legislative Assembly on 20 April to ask for a declaration of war against Austria; the decree passed easily the next day, with only seven deputies dissenting.[40] Lafayette, who had returned to military service in December 1791, favored the war, arguing that it would strengthen the constitutional monarchy. Marie Antoinette also supported the war, because she hoped that Francis II would help to restore the French monarchy.[41] On the other side, Robespierre and Marat, the editor of *L'Ami du Peuple*, continued to oppose the conflict as dissension increased between the moderate and radical factions in the Legislative Assembly.

Meanwhile, the French army, marching into the Austrian Netherlands in the spring of 1792, soon met defeat. Suffering from a lack of discipline and qualified officers, many of the troops fell into a state of disorder and fled across the frontier. Under the Ancien Régime, the officers had come from the nobility, and many of them had chosen to emigrate in 1789. In addition, the new middle-class officers had no experience of commanding men, who had come to think of themselves as equal.[42] It was an altogether unworkable situation for waging war against experienced European forces.

Despite the military setback, in May the Girondin-led leadership in the assembly passed several decrees to limit the king's power. The first one, which he approved, abolished the king's constitutional guard of twelve hundred infantry and six hundred cavalry; he was left with nine hundred Swiss guards. The other two decrees, which the king vetoed, ordered the deportation of non-juring priests and called for twenty thousand provincial National Guardsmen (fédérés) to come to Paris to protect the Legislative Assembly. The Girondin-led ministry and assembly felt that they needed protection, because the Parisian National Guard had become filled with radicals from the sections. The original sixty electoral districts of Paris had been replaced earlier by the National Assembly with forty-eight so-called sections.[43]

After Minister of the Interior Jean Roland had sent an open letter to the king on 13 June, asking him to approve the decrees on the non-juring priests and the fédérés or else expect violence, Louis XVI responded by dismissing his Girondin ministers on 16 June. Violence did indeed follow very soon thereafter on 20 June, when the Parisian sections, joined by crowds along the way, marched toward the Tuileries palace. Although the king was not harmed, he was humiliated and forced to put on a red liberty cap, the "Phrygian bonnet" of the revolutionaries, and the crowds remained until nightfall.[44]

While the Girondins had been busy working behind the scenes to reinstate their ministers, the Jacobins, led by Robespierre, Danton, Hébert, and Santerre, had consolidated public support and gained strength in the Paris sections. The city was filled with unrest due to food shortages and military defeats, six hundred fédérés from Marseille had arrived, and there were reports that the Austrians and Prussians led by the Duke of Brunswick were preparing to invade France. The situation had become untenable, causing the Legislative Assembly to engage in intense debates about the best course to follow. On 1 August the arrival of the Brunswick Manifesto only served to increase the anxiety of Parisians and deputies alike. The duke had announced that he intended to rescue the royal family, and furthermore, if they were harmed, his troops would destroy the city "by fire and sword." To add to this alarming turn of events, the Paris sections urged the assembly to remove Louis XVI from power by 9 August, or "face the wrath of Paris." Then, to emphasize their influence, three representatives from each section were chosen to form a new Commune and an insurrection was planned for 10 August.

Members of the new Commune entered the Hotel de Ville, where the old Commune was in session, on the night of 9–10 August, dismissing all of the officials who opposed their aims. Santerre, the main organizer of the sections, took command of the National Guard and proceeded to withdraw the troops from the Tuileries area. The royal family, now only protected by the nine hundred Swiss guards and three hundred volunteers of the Order of Chevaliers de St. Louis, withdrew from the palace and entered the quarters of the Legislative Assembly, where they hoped for safety. Left without any instructions, the Swiss guards were overwhelmed by the armed crowds pushing their way into the Tuileries on the morning of 10 August, and only three hundred of them were able to escape. The insurrectionists moved from the palace to the nearby quarters of the Legislative Assembly, where the defenseless deputies had little choice but to accede to the new Commune's demands. They agreed, therefore, to suspend Louis XVI from office and to imprison him and the royal family in the Temple, as well as to call a national convention to replace the Legislative Assembly and to write a new constitution.[45]

In the midst of "this grand commotion," according to contemporary witnesses, the assembly had reacted in a calm and orderly manner to carry out the Commune's orders, reasoning wisely that refusing to do so would have resulted in further violence.[46] While the Legislative Assembly had moved slowly in deciding on the proper position of the king, the Parisian sections and political clubs had grown tired of waiting and had acted to force a decision. Moved to action by the threat of foreign invasion, the Parisian sections had shown that their power was not to be ignored, and that power would only grow stronger in the days ahead.

Following the events of 10 August 1792, the Legislative Assembly appointed a provisional executive council and announced that elections for the National Convention would be held in September. The Girondin ministers Roland, Clavière, and Servan, who had been dismissed earlier by the king, were recalled to their former positions; Jacques Danton joined them as the new minister of justice. The selection of Danton was meant to placate the Parisians, among whom this man of the people was very popular.

Describing the frenetic pace of events in 1791 and 1792, Manon Roland wrote, "We are living through ten years in twenty-four hours; events and emotions are jumbled together and follow each other with a singular rapidity." The natural unfolding of days, weeks, and months seemed to have vanished as surely as the traditional order of the Ancien Régime.[47]

It was during that tumultuous year of 1792 that Vigée-LeBrun's name had been added to the list of émigrés. That August her husband had made a formal request to the Legislative Assembly for the removal of her name, but his plea had been denied. LeBrun worried that his properties might be confiscated and he began to fear for his own safety. With the fall of the monarchy and a newly elected National Convention, the laws regarding émigrés had grown more restrictive; their property could revert legally to the revolutionary government. Yet, despite the possible danger, LeBrun published in October a fervent defense of his wife's conduct in a twenty-two-page pamphlet titled "Précis historique de la vie de la citoyenne LeBrun, peintre." He explained that she had gone to Italy only to pursue her art, not as an émigré, which was an outright lie, and he reminded readers that Vigée-LeBrun had been among those artists who had donated their jewels to the National Assembly in a patriotic gesture in September 1789. This probably was not true either; she made no mention of it in her memoir. LeBrun wrote that she had planned the trip to Italy several times, but due to the pressure of her work, she had been unable to leave. Explaining that his wife had left France with regret, he wrote that she needed peaceful conditions in order to work: "The arts are friends of peace and silence."[48]

Citing the decrees of 1792 that allowed persons to leave France for Italy, LeBrun emphasized that his wife had traveled only to Italy and that she even had submitted a painting to the Salon of 1791.[49] LeBrun also denounced as lies the rumors about Vigée-LeBrun and Calonne, the former finance minister, insisting that their home had served as a sort of *lycée* open to all talents, a meeting place for artists and composers, rather than a place where aristocrats gathered. He declared that both he and his wife had worked hard to achieve their situation and that his only riches consisted of their homes and gallery on the rue de Cléry and rue du Gros Chênet. Finally, he praised Vigée-LeBrun's great artistic talent and her untiring efforts to become one of the greatest French painters.[50]

LeBrun's persuasive, if not altogether true, arguments on his wife's behalf had been put forth as part of his survival strategy during an increasingly uncertain period. Following the publication of "Précis historique," LeBrun made another appeal to the government to allow Vigée-LeBrun to be listed among artists traveling outside of France for study purposes; again, his petition was rejected. In November 1793, LeBrun was imprisoned, but he was released a short time later. Etienne Vigée, the artist's brother, was less fortunate. Also arrested in 1793 and imprisoned at Port-Libre, he would remain there until July 1794.[51]

As conditions became more dangerous in 1793 and 1794 for anyone thought to have aristocratic connections, LeBrun took a decisive step to ensure his own safety. In June 1794 he divorced his absent wife, suing on grounds of abandonment.[52] French civil law had changed, so that divorce became possible after 1792 on a number of grounds, including desertion or separation for a period of at least two years. Divorce also was justified if a spouse had gone into exile or disappeared.[53] Wives or husbands of émigrés frequently used divorce to protect themselves or their family's property from confiscation by the revolutionary government.[54] Since

LeBrun and his wife corresponded regularly during her period of exile, the charge of "abandonment" was obviously false. However, LeBrun had felt more than usually threatened in 1794, because he was under investigation by a special commission. According to an official report, an alleged monarchist plot implicating LeBrun concerned the removal of an inscription from one of his wife's portraits. He had gone to the Château de St. Cloud to delete a dedication to Marie Antoinette, which appeared on a pastel copy of Vigée-LeBrun's portrait of Paisiello. This particular copy had been found hidden in the dauphin's bedroom in May 1794, along with her portrait of the dauphin, Louis Charles, who was at that time still imprisoned.[55] While LeBrun was under investigation for this matter, he had acted prudently in divorcing his wife, a known and unrepentant royalist. While we cannot be sure, it is probable that LeBrun's calculated action at this time, when the Terror was at its zenith, saved his life.

LeBrun had continued his various art-related activities between 1792 and 1794. His "Réflexions sur le Muséum National," a pro-republican essay concerning the formation of a museum housing the world's treasures, focused on the composition and arrangement of a national museum suitable for Paris, "the capital of the universe."[56] His publications in 1793 (*Observations sur le Muséum National*) and 1794 (*Quelques Idées sur la Disposition, l'Arrangement, et la Décoration du Muséum National*) influenced the transition of the Louvre from a royal to a national museum.[57]

Both LeBrun and his friend Jacques-Louis David were active supporters of the Republic and served on political committees in the early 1790s. They both favored the northern genre paintings championed and displayed by LeBrun in his gallery. It has been suggested by art historian Carol S. Eliel that their support of Dutch painting had an ideological basis, that the "northern genre painting was a democratic rather than aristocratic art form . . . a politics of style." Pointing out that seventeenth-century Dutch artists were "not controlled by royal or aristocratic patrons or academies," she found that there were aspects of that society that "approached the model republic to which revolutionary France aspired."[58] This convenient connection between art and politics is not surprising during the upheaval caused by the revolution. On LeBrun's part, it is instructive to note his accommodation efforts under all of the governments that existed in France from 1775 until his death in 1813. While his preference for the seventeenth-century northern genre artists comes through in his writings as genuine, his support of the different forms of government appears to have been strategically determined.

For her part, Vigée-LeBrun accepted her husband's actions during the revolution as necessary for his survival and the preservation of their property. She made no mention of the divorce in her memoir and, in fact, returned after her exile to their home in Paris, where she was welcomed with a surprise party by LeBrun and other family members.[59] She also made no mention in her memoir about her brother's acts of opportunism during the revolution. Like his sister, Vigée had prospered under the monarchy, yet in 1793 he had written and recited a rabidly antimonarchist poem, "Ode à la liberté." He also occupied a post from 1795 to 1799 responsible for selling off the émigrés' property. A successful poet and playwright under the Ancien Régime, Vigée had become an ardent revolutionary writer and official. Later he evolved into an opportunistic poet lauding Napoleon, and then an official reader under Louis XVIII, the brother of Louis XVI. In 1802 Vigée had replaced Jean François Laharpe as the chair of literature at the Athénée. A talented orator and diction teacher, he was "a strange combination of levity and bombast," and, above all, a skillful survivor.[60] It is likely that Vigée-LeBrun considered her brother's actions much the same as she did her husband's—simply a means of survival during a difficult period.

NOTES

1. Donald Greer, *The Incidence of Emigration During the French Revolution* (Cambridge, Mass.: Harvard University Press, 1951); James Roberts, *The Counter-Revolution in France, 1787–1830* (New York: St. Martin's Press, 1990); Ghislain de Diesbach, *Histoire de l'Emigration, 1789–1814* (Paris: Librairie Académique Perrin, 1984, revised ed.).

2. Greer, *The Incidence of Emigration*, 27, 30.

3. Greer, *The Incidence of Emigration*, 33–35.

4. Roberts, *The Counter-Revolution in France*, xi.

5. Greer, *The Incidence of Emigration*, 29; Roberts, *The Counter-Revolution in France*, 6.

6. Peter Fritzsche, *Stranded in the Present: Modern Time and the Melancholy of History* (Cambridge, Mass.: Harvard University Press, 2004).

7. The other women artists were Anne Vallayer-Coster, Marie-Thérèse Wien, and Adélaide Labille-Guiard.

8. Michel Gallet, "La Maison de Mme. Vigée-LeBrun, rue du Gros Chênet," *Gazette de Beaux Arts* (November 1960): 282.

9. Elisabeth Louise Vigée-LeBrun, *Souvenirs*, 3 vols. (Paris: Librairie de H. Fournier, 1835–1837), I: 184–85.

10. Vigée-LeBrun, *Souvenirs*, I: 195.

11. Vigée-LeBrun, *Souvenirs*, I: 199–201.

12. Vigée-LeBrun, *Souvenirs*, II: 20, 39. See also Mary D. Sheriff, *The Exceptional Woman: Elisabeth Vigée-LeBrun and the Cultural Politics of Art* (Chicago: University of Chicago Press, 1996), 229–30.

13. Vigée-LeBrun, *Souvenirs*, II: 59.

14. Joseph Baillio, *Elisabeth Vigée-LeBrun*, 1755–1842, exhibition catalogue, Kimbell Art Museum (Fort Worth, Tex.: Kimbell Art Museum, 1982), 99.

15. Vigée-LeBrun, *Souvenirs*, II: 136.

16. See Criticism of Salon of 1791, anthologized in *Collection Deloynes* (Paris: Bibliothèque Nationale, Cabinet des Estampes), XVII, 10, 39–40; Baillio, *Elisabeth Vigée-LeBrun*, 95–96.

17. See Bette W. Oliver, *From Royal to National: The Louvre Museum and the Bibliothèque Nationale* (Lanham, Md.: Lexington Books, 2007).

18. Vigée-LeBrun, *Souvenirs*, II: 218–30; Baillio, *Elisabeth Vigée-LeBrun*, 104–6.

19. Baillio, *Elisabeth Vigée-LeBrun*, 53; Simon Schama, *Citizens: A Chronicle of the French Revolution* (New York: Alfred A Knopf, 1989), 215.

20. Vigée-LeBrun, *Souvenirs*, I: 210–13.

21. Baillio, *Elisabeth Vigée-LeBrun*, 51–53.

22. Vigée-LeBrun, *Souvenirs*, I: 159.

23. Vigée-LeBrun, *Souvenirs*, II: 220.

24. Vigée-LeBrun, *Souvenirs*, II: 259.

25. Henri Troyat, *Catherine the Great* (New York: Berkeley Books, 1981), 372.

26. Troyat, *Catherine the Great*, 375.

27. Baillio, *Elisabeth Vigée-LeBrun*, 118, 119, 110.

28. Baillio, *Elisabeth Vigée-LeBrun*, 19. The two paintings were "Lady Hamilton as a Sibyl" (1791–1792) and "The Artist's Daughter Playing a Guitar" (1797).

29. Unpublished letter to "Monsieur LeBrun/Artiste Célèbre Rue de Gros Chênet, Paris," dated 29 January 1801, from Moscow, in *Papiers Tripier Le Franc*, Carton 52, Dossier II, Liasse I (Paris: Bibliothèque Doucet); Vigée-LeBrun, *Souvenirs*, III: 62–64.

30. Vigée-LeBrun, *Souvenirs*, III: 75–77.

31. Vigée-LeBrun, *Souvenirs*, III: 128.

32. Vigée-LeBrun, *Souvenirs*, III: 134–35.

33. Owen Connelly, *French Revolution/Napoleonic Era* (New York: Holt, Rinehart and Winston, 1979), 108–10.

34. François-Nicolas-Louis Buzot, *Mémoires de F.-N.-L. Buzot, Membre de l'Assemblée Constituante et Député à la Convention Nationale par le Departement de l'Eure, Année 1793*, N. A. F. 1730, 74–76 (Paris: Bibliothèque Nationale, Dept. des Manuscrits).

35. For a detailed discussion of the king's failed escape, see Timothy Tackett, *When the King Took Flight* (Cambridge, Mass./London: Harvard University Press, 2003).

36. Tackett, *When the King Took Flight*, 141–42.

37. Connelly, *French Revolution*, 112–15.

38. Connelly, *French Revolution*, 114–15.

39. Eloise Ellery, *Brissot De Warville: A Study in the History of the French Revolution* (Boston and New York: Houghton Mifflin, 1915; reprinted New York: Burt Franklin, 1970), 228, 236–38; M. J. Sydenham, *The Girondins* (London: University of London, Athlone Press, 1961), 101.

40. Ellery, *Brissot de Warville*, 250–51, *Moniteur* (April 20, 1792).

41. Connelly, *French Revolution*, 116.

42. Connelly, *French Revolution*, 117–18; David Andress, *The Terror: The Merciless War for Freedom in Revolutionary France* (New York: Farrar, Straus and Giroux, 2005), 73.

43. Connelly, *French Revolution*, 118–19.

44. Connelly, *French Revolution*, 119.

45. Connelly, *French Revolution*, 120–22; David P. Jordan, *The King's Trial: Louis XVI vs. the French Revolution* (Berkeley: University of California Press, 1979, 2004), 41.

46. C. A. Dauban, ed., *Mémoires Inédits de Pétion et Mémoires de Buzot & de Barbaroux accompagnés de Notes Inédites de Buzot et de nombreux documents inédits sur Barbaroux, Buzot, Brissot, etc.* (Paris: Henri Plon, 1866), 366–68.

47. Cl. Perroud, ed., *Lettres de Madame Roland*, vol. 2, *1788–1793* (Paris, 1902), II: 325, letter to Henri Bancal dated 11 July 1792.

48. Jean-Baptiste Pierre LeBrun, *Précis Historique de la Vie de la Citoyenne LeBrun, peintre* (Paris, 1793), 16, 17 (Paris: Bibliothèque Doucet).

49. LeBrun, *Précis Historique*, 19, 20. Loi du Avril 1792, relative aux biens des Émigrés, Art. VI; Loi du 18 Octobre, 1792, Art. I; Loi du 28 Mars 1793, Art. VIII, Section IV.

50. LeBrun, *Précis Historique*, 11, 12, 15, 8.

51. Baillio, *Elisabeth Vigée-LeBrun*, 14.

52. *Papiers Tripier Lefranc*, Carton 51, No. 27804-6 and No. 27272 (Paris: Bibliothèque Doucet).

53. Roderick Phillips, *Putting Asunder: A History of Divorce in Western Society* (New York: Cambridge University Press, 1988), 162–63, 173.

54. James F. Traer, *Marriage and the Family in Eighteenth-Century France* (Ithaca, N.Y.: Cornell University Press, 1980), 132–33.

55. Baillio, *Elisabeth Vigée-LeBrun*, 95.

56. Jean-Baptiste Pierre LeBrun, *Réflexions sur le Muséum National* (Paris, 1792), 5 (Paris: Bibliothèque Doucet, 8 F 1664).

57. LeBrun, *Observations sur le Muséum National* (Paris, 1793) and *Quelques Idées sur la Disposition, l'Arrangement, et la Décoration du Muséum National* (Paris, 1794) (Paris: Bibliothèque Doucet, 8 F999 and 8 F990). For a detailed discussion of the transition to a national museum, see Bette W. Oliver, *From Royal to National: The Louvre Museum and the Bibliothèque Nationale* (Lanham, Md.: Lexington Books, 2007).

58. Carol S. Eliel, "Genre Painting During the Revolution and the Goût Hollandais" in *1789: French Art during the Revolution* exhibition catalogue, edited by Alan Wintermute (New York: Colnaghi, 1989), 49, 50.

59. Gilberte Emile-Mâle, "Jean-Baptiste Pierre LeBrun (1748–1813): Son Rôle Dans l'Histoire de la Restauration des Tableaux du Louvre" (391–417) in *Paris et Île-de-France* 8, 382; Vigée-LeBrun, *Souvenirs*, III: 130; Baillio, *Elisabeth Vigée-LeBrun*, 15. Vigée-Le-Brun later asked LeBrun to return her dowry and began using her maiden name in legal contracts.

60. Baillio, *Elisabeth Vigée-LeBrun*, 32–33.

THREE

French Émigrés in the United States

While the largest exodus from France occurred in 1793 and 1794, there were, in addition to those who left in 1789, other early émigrés who chose to depart with no intention of returning. This group of émigrés, in fact, wanted nothing to do with the revolutionary government; they wished to leave their troubled country far behind and settle in the United States. Unlike the monarchists who had left in 1789, they formed a diverse group, often politically neutral, which was looking for employment, adventure, or for a small group of aristocrats, some sort of a wilderness refuge. They were voluntary émigrés, many of whom had lost their jobs because the revolution had upset the old order: artisans, merchants, domestic servants, as well as non-juring priests. The group also included some conservative aristocrats, members of the Compagnie des Vingt-Quatre, or "the 24," led by the Marquis de Lezay-Marnésia. They had little use for the new order of equality promised by the revolutionary government and hoped to create an ideal version of pre-revolutionary France in the Ohio wilderness. In effect, they envisioned an agricultural settlement of paternalistic landowners living in peace and order. These aristocrats would be among the approximately one thousand French citizens who sailed to the United States in 1790.

The opportunity to leave France and begin new lives in America, specifically in the Ohio Valley wilderness, was provided by an American land company, the Scioto Company, which had opened its Paris office in August 1789. While the Scioto Co. would later become notorious as an example of an American land company operating under false pretenses to take advantage of French citizens, in August 1789 it was seen as a means of escaping the unsettled conditions in France.[1] The Scioto Co. *Prospectus* had been designed to appeal not only to potential emigrants but to investors as well, even including advice on the probable costs involved for such items as seeds, livestock, and agricultural tools.[2]

The *Prospectus* also sought to reassure the emigrants that they would not be isolated in their new settlement. Consequently, the French public responded enthusiastically to this opportunity, and a veritable "Scioto-mania" swept over Paris. Citizens of differing social, economic, and regional backgrounds were eager to buy acreage located in what they imagined to be a natural paradise in southern Ohio. They could not know that, rather than buying title to a specific amount of land, they would only be buying a preemption. They also had no idea that living on the Ohio frontier would be a severe challenge for those accustomed to living in cities, where necessities were readily available.[3]

The Scioto Co. had been organized in 1787 by a group of American speculators, who sent Joel Barlow to Paris to serve as their agent. Barlow, however, was not well suited to the task, because he was a poet, not a businessman. Therefore, he enlisted the help of an English adventurer, William Playfair, who was familiar with French laws and customs, to help him sell the Ohio lands to French citizens. They formed the Compagnie du Scioto in August of 1789 and enjoyed a brisk business initially. It was only later, when reports from the disgruntled émigrés reached France, that the company became mired in scandal.

As mentioned earlier, the purchasers of the Ohio land were diverse. A selection of letters addressed to the Duc d'Eprémesnil, one of the original twenty-four large investors, provides representative solicitations from persons eager to leave France.[4] Several unemployed young men described their various skills, such as mathematics, agriculture, law, and architecture, which could be useful in America. Another unemployed provincial wrote about wanting to help his family financially and portrayed himself as "having a good strong constitution." Laborers stressed their willingness to work hard or their honesty. In addition to the men, there were women—single, married, separated, or widowed—who also hoped for better lives overseas. One mother of four children wrote that she and her husband needed the means to emigrate, because they could no longer earn or save money in France.[5]

The Compagnie du Scioto office was busy with transactions between the fall of 1789 and the spring of 1790. Most of the purchasers in November and December 1789 were Parisians, who bought parcels of land ranging from fifty to seven hundred acres, most paying half the price at time of purchase and the balance by a specified later date. According to the notary, M. Farmain, sales had increased to five or six a day by January 1790. The purchases of wealthier customers, including members of "the 24," ranged from one thousand to twenty-four thousand acres in 1790.[6] An examination of notarial records in the Archives Nationales includes numerous examples of these land sales.[7] Not surprisingly, aristocrats were responsible for the larger purchases. The Duc d'Eprémesnil, for example, bought ten thousand acres for 30,000 livres, while Lezay-Marnésia bought twenty thousand acres for 60,000 livres. Another aristocrat, Lochet Duchainet, bought twenty-four thousand acres for 72,000 livres.[8] On the other hand, many of the emigrants, such as contract laborers and domestic servants, could not afford to purchase any amount of land. By January 1790, approximately one hundred and fifty thousand acres of land had been sold by the Compagnie du Scioto. Only after their arrival in the United States would the French buyers discover that, due to a surveying error, they did not possess clear titles to their lands, which actually belonged to the Ohio Company.

The first group of four hundred men, women, and children to depart from France, accompanied by a French agent, M. Boulogne, gathered at Le Havre in January 1790. Composed mostly of middle-class Parisians, a few aristocrats, and some contract laborers, this group waited for over a month before the five packet ships arrived. Since the ships departed from France at different times, they would arrive at the northeastern ports in the United States separately, thus adding to the confusion of the French travelers and the American agents assigned to meet them. After voyages lasting two to three months, the ships, filled with approximately one thousand Frenchmen, arrived in Alexandria, Philadelphia, and New York between May and October. Depending on the voyagers' experiences, the reports trickling back to France were greatly varied in tone. Their experiences after landing, however, were not optimal and did not bode well for the success of the Ohio venture.[9]

The experiences of the first group serve as an example of the frustrations encountered after their arrival in the United States. When they landed at Alexandria, Virginia, on 1 May 1790, the assigned agent, Colonel David Franks, was not there to meet them. He apparently had tired of waiting for them, reasoning that they must have landed elsewhere. The French, stranded in a foreign city, were treated well enough by the citizens of Alexandria, but they also were warned that the Scioto Co. was not reliable and that "savages" awaited them in the isolated Ohio wilderness. Some of the group became so discouraged that they decided to remain in Alexandria or to go on to Philadelphia, where they could join other French émigrés. A few even decided to return to France. The rest of the group, however, was determined to wait for someone from the Scioto Co. to arrive and guide them to their lands in Ohio. Increasingly annoyed by the delays, they even wrote a letter to President George Washington, who hastened to assure them that they would not be abandoned.[10]

Finally at the end of May, Major Guion arrived to escort the emigrants to Ohio, but he realized that he faced a dilemma. He feared serious disorder if another ship arrived before he departed with the first group; however, he had been warned that if the French settlers arrived in the Ohio wilderness too soon, they would find a shortage of provisions.[11] Major Guion decided to take a chance and leave Alexandria before any more

French emigrants arrived. The first group had already insisted that the Scioto Co. reimburse them for expenses incurred while they waited in Alexandria. After the Scioto Co. agreed to their demands, the group final-ly departed on 29 June, escorted by Major Guion and James Backus, who had made arrangements for necessary accommodations on the journey to Ohio.[12]

Travel by wagons in the heat of the summer, up and down hills and mountains, was filled with discomforts, especially for those used to living in cities. The frequent rain showers increased their discomfort and led to delays. Occasionally a wagon hit a rough patch and turned over, causing its inhabitants to sustain injuries. To add to their miseries, the provisions and accommodations did not always match expectations, and the compa-ny's credit was not worth much at this time. If the emigrants attempted to purchase items, they were overcharged, and two of them were even ar-rested for debt, only to be rescued later by their friends.[13]

The first group had traveled from Alexandria to Winchester and Red Stone, and then to the mouth of the Buffalo Creek, the current location of Wellsburg, West Virginia. There they waited for flat boats to take them down the Ohio River. Occasionally these "arks" would become grounded, causing further delays. Nevertheless, the passengers were be-ginning to feel optimistic and excited, because they were finally ap-proaching their destination. Reaching the mouth of the Great Kanawha River toward mid-October, the French were encouraged by the pristine beauty of the autumn woods surrounding them—a "paradise of nature" that truly matched their expectations.[14]

The land for their settlement had been cleared and cabins built, but the area appeared less than attractive to the emigrants. They saw before them "two parallel rows of log cabins, each row some three hundred feet in length, and forming streets parallel with the river." Spaces between the cabins had been left for cross streets at one-hundred-foot intervals, and a blockhouse filled each corner of the rectangle. Despite their disappoint-ment in the accommodations, the settlers proceeded to move into the rustic cabins, determined to deal with whatever challenges faced them.[15]

The furniture and various other fine objects that the wealthier French had brought with them (now conserved in the Gallipolis Museum) would be of little use in the wilderness. Their fine paintings, inlaid furniture, silver chandeliers, and expensive clocks offered proof of their misconcep-tions about frontier life. Those who had been poor in France, however, had not brought much with them, and thus found it easier to accept the rusticity of their new homes. Only a month after their arrival, in Novem-ber 1790, the first marriage took place in the settlement that would be named Gallipolis, the city of the Gauls.[16]

The Scioto Co. had assured the settlers that necessary provisions would be supplied to them until their first crop was ready for harvest. Several members of the company, which was short of money, paid for some of the food themselves and helped to establish a store where the settlers could buy necessities. Since the French had no prior experience in clearing land, felling trees, or farming, however, they found themselves woefully unprepared for survival in the wilderness. Fortunately, they were able to plant gardens and cultivate grape vines successfully, which helped to improve their situation. They also were able to buy vegetables and pork from boats passing by (except when the river was blocked by ice), and hunters helped to supply meat.[17]

However, the settlers faced other serious problems. The Scioto Co. *Prospectus* had not described the area as isolated, nor had it issued any warnings of the presence of unfriendly Indians. Despite treaties, Indian raids occurred nearby in 1789, 1790, and 1791. The Gallipolis settlers even participated in a regional offensive against the Indians in July 1791, but it was not successful. Only in August 1794 were the Indians in the region subdued by Mad Anthony Wayne and his troops at the Battle of Fallen Timbers.[18]

Another vexing problem facing the French was the matter of gaining clear titles to their land. Due to a geographical miscalculation, Gallipolis had been built on land that actually belonged to the Ohio Co. The settlers, therefore, were expected to pay again for their land, this time to the Ohio Co. Not surprisingly, some of the settlers refused to do this, choosing instead to leave Gallipolis for other cities, notably Philadelphia or New Orleans, or to move to land in nearby Kentucky or Illinois. For those who remained in Gallipolis, the payment problem with the Ohio Co. would not be resolved until 1795.[19]

Meanwhile, "the 24," the group of French aristocrats who had bought large tracts of land early in 1790, had never intended to live among the other French settlers in Gallipolis. When they arrived in late October, Lezay-Marnésia and de Barth, two leaders of the group, chose to remain at nearby Fort Harmar in Marietta. That November several members of "the 24," accompanied by guides, explored areas along the Scioto and Ohio Rivers, looking for land that might be suitable for a large plantation. They returned favorably impressed with what they had seen; however, in their absence Lezay-Marnésia had traveled to Pittsburgh on business and apparently nothing could be decided until he returned.[20] His eccentric behavior had been duly noted by Americans in the area, one of whom described Lezay-Marnésia as "the last of the imbeciles." He could not agree with the other members of "the 24" on much of anything, and he finally announced on 15 November 1790 that he was leaving the association to join citizens in Marietta, who planned on forming another settlement.[21]

The colony of Marietta, situated near Fort Harmar on the Muskingum River, had been established in 1788 by General Putnam and other veterans of the American Revolution. It had been named in honor of the French queen, Marie Antoinette, in gratitude for French assistance during the revolution. Considering the rustic frontier conditions both at Fort Harmar and Marietta, the French aristocrats, along with their families and servants, were not satisfied with their accommodations. General Arthur St. Clair, the governor of the Northwest Territory, opened his house to de Barth as a sign of respect for his age; in addition, de Barth's "cave" also was welcome to share his residence. De Barth's contract workers were instructed to clear a tract of land that he had purchased near Marietta. According to reports, however, they proved unreliable and were often found hunting or drinking whiskey instead of working.[22]

Lezay-Marnésia, meanwhile, continued to annoy those around him with his eccentric behavior. According to a letter dated 15 November 1790, written to M. le chevalier de Bouffers in France, Lezay-Marnésia had been visited at dinner by "the Queen of the Hurons," who wished to honor him as "the French chief." In his *Lettres écrits des rives de l'Ohio*, Lezay-Marnésia praised the Indians as "children of nature," finding them superior to "representatives of the civilized world." At this time he also continued to write to friends in France, urging them to join him, and in 1791 the last group of 120 French emigrants arrived in Philadelphia.[23]

Lezay-Marnésia's son, Albert, did not agree with his father about the superiority of the Indians or about living in Marietta. To him, the "savages" seemed to be "disfigured by paint and bizarre tatoos," and their table manners were "disgusting." Likewise, he did not enjoy living in the wilderness. "We are reduced to living the life of the Savages," he wrote, "surrounded by a rare population of Americans, true savages themselves."[24]

If some of the aristocrats were less than satisfied, those settlers who had remained in Gallipolis were still trying to gain clear titles to the lands they had purchased from the Scioto Co. Their situation had become even more complicated since William Playfair of the French branch of the company had absconded with the funds meant to pay the U.S. Congress. In addition, between October 1791 and January 1792, a "speculative orgy" had erupted in New York. William Duer, a member of the Scioto Co. who had been instrumental in the purchase of land from Congress, had been imprisoned for debt. Duer, who had worked under Alexander Hamilton in the Treasury Department, had used his access to information so that he and others could speculate on government bonds. When their scheme failed, many investors lost a great deal of money, causing a financial panic. Duer could not pay back the money he had borrowed; thus he was disgraced and imprisoned in March 1792, and he would die there in 1799.[25]

Despite this setback, the settlers in Gallipolis persisted in their efforts. One of them, Jean Gervais, discussed the situation with a respected French lawyer in Philadelphia and together they prepared a petition to the U.S. Congress. They asked for a grant of land for the Gallipolis settlers, who, in return, would cede to the United States their claims on the Scioto and Ohio companies.[26]

On 3 March 1795 the U.S. Congress responded to the petition by issuing the French Grant. Its terms declared that French settlers older than eighteen residing in Gallipolis on 1 November 1795 would be granted twenty-four thousand acres of land in the southern part of present-day Scioto County, located downstream from Gallipolis on the north shore of the Ohio River. Rather than causing an exodus from Gallipolis, however, the grant only attracted approximately sixteen of the original settlers between 1796 and 1801.[27]

In December 1795, those French settlers still remaining in Gallipolis asked the Ohio Co. to give them the land that they had originally paid for in Paris in 1789. While the company did not consent to do that, it did agree to sell them "those sections of its land, including the town of Gallipolis and the adjacent improved lots, at the nominal price of a dollar and a quarter an acre." The settlers also were allowed to share in the Ohio Co.'s Donation Trust on the Muskingum River.[28]

Approximately one hundred French families lived in Gallipolis at this time. That number did not include members of "the 24," who had moved to less isolated locations. The Duc d'Eprémesnil, one of the group's most prominent leaders, had not even bothered to travel to the Ohio wilderness, choosing instead to authorize an agent, Bancel de Coufoulens, to exchange the Scioto Co. tract for acreage in Maine. As it turned out, however, the Duc d'Esprémesnil had delayed his journey to the United States for far too long, and by the time he was ready to leave in 1794, he was prohibited from doing so. Instead, like so many other aristocrats during the Terror, he was arrested and executed.[29]

The Marquis de Lezay-Marnésia fared somewhat better, although he never realized his dream of creating a colony based on the paternalistic ideals of the Ancien Régime. He had left Ohio, along with his son Albert, and moved to Pittsburgh, where he proceeded to initiate another plan for a four-hundred-acre settlement on the Monongahela River, which he called Asilum. In 1791 he attempted to attract both the Duc d'Eprémesnil and Bernardin de Saint-Pierre to the project, but failed to impress them. Discouraged again, he decided to return to France.[30] Before he finally departed from the United States, however, Lezay-Marnésia became involved in yet another plan to create a settlement, that of Nouvelle-Bourbon in Missouri. He assured his associates that he would continue to participate in the project even after he had returned to France.[31]

Arriving in France in early 1792, Lezay-Marnésia, like the Duc d'Eprémesnil before him, was arrested and imprisoned in March 1794. However, he did not share the fate of his compatriot. Instead, thanks to the events of 9 Thermidor, and sheer good luck, he was released from prison. Apparently not feeling secure enough to remain in France, he left again, this time taking refuge at Jacques Necker's home in Switzerland.

Lezay-Marnésia, a survivor in spite of himself, would die a natural death at Besançon in 1800.[32]

While Lezay-Marnésia and the other members of "the 24" felt that they had been cheated by the Scioto Co. and had chosen to depart for other venues, those settlers who remained in Gallipolis worked to improve their situation. In 1793 the French population numbered three hundred plus forty soldiers, but by 1802 a visitor to the area found only 160 French inhabitants, and the tax register of 1806 listed only 16 French names out of a total of 145. The "Americanization" of Gallipolis had begun, even as the town attracted settlers from other areas of the United States. An act of Congress in April 1802 naturalized the French inhabitants of Gallipolis, and in 1803 the Territory of the Northwest became the state of Ohio.[33] Gallipolis bears the distinction of being the only French colony in the United States to have succeeded. Others, such as Asylum on the Susquehanna River, only flourished briefly before their inhabitants chose to return to France in 1802, when it became safe to do so.[34]

The fall of the monarchy in 1792 and subsequent events had led to another wave of émigrés seeking safety outside of France. This group, however, did not choose to leave voluntarily like those in 1789 and 1790; thus, they did not have time to make careful plans before their departure. Also, unlike those voluntary émigrés, the second wave left in order to survive, and most planned to return to France as soon as it became safe to do so. Many of those who left between 1792 and 1794 had participated in the early days of the revolution and had been considered patriots, even national leaders. The Marquis de Lafayette, for example, called the "Hero of Two Worlds" by his admirers, left France for England, but he was captured en route by the Austrians and imprisoned at Olmütz, where he remained until 1797.

The second wave of émigrés was motivated by the number of unforeseen and frightening events after August 1792, which provided evidence that the radicals had gained control of the government. In addition, elections for the National Convention had favored the candidates of the new Paris Commune, notably Robespierre, Danton (who had relinquished his position as minister of justice), and Marat. Robespierre worked to undermine the Girondin faction, even denouncing its leaders in a speech to the Convention on 4 September. For her part, Manon Roland blamed Robespierre for instigating the so-called September massacres in which more than eleven hundred prisoners were killed by roaming crowds that invaded Paris prisons. Marat, in his newspaper, *L'Ami du Peuple*, had contributed to the mayhem by warning of enemies hiding in their midst who were preparing to attack Paris. Then, on 29 October, Minister of the Interior Roland, in a speech to the National Convention, indicted the Commune for usurpation of power and acts of terrorism; he went so far as to accuse Robespierre of aiming to become a dictator.[35]

In November 1792, the discovery of the king's secret iron safe furnished proof that Louis XVI had conspired against the revolution with Mirabeau and foreign governments. In addition, Roland was accused of having removed documents from the safe that might have compromised the Girondins, and he was also suspected of having conducted secret negotiations with the English government. This development served to intensify the existing factional divisions within the Convention, but it was the king's trial from 11 December 1792 to 15 January 1793 that definitively signaled the ascendancy of the radicals within the Convention. While the Girondin deputies favored a trial and possible exile for Louis XVI, the Jacobins called for his execution. After the king was found guilty of conspiracy against the nation by the unanimous vote of the 693 deputies who were present, the Girondin deputies proposed a national plebiscite on the king's sentence. They reasoned that such a referendum would show conservative support for the king in the provinces and among the French peasantry, but their proposal met defeat. Consequently, by a vote 387 to 334, the Convention decided that Louis XVI must be executed for his crimes, and on 21 January 1793, he was guillotined.[36]

Although many of the two hundred Girondin deputies in the National Convention finally had voted for the execution of the king, their call for a referendum on his sentence had not helped their cause. After Roland had been denounced in the Convention by Robespierre and even accused of treasonous activities, he resigned from his position of interior minister on 23 January 1793, to be replaced by Dominique Garat. Earlier, in December, Manon Roland had been ordered to appear before the Convention, where she had been accused of involvement in a royalist conspiracy. She made it clear in a letter to her friend Lanthenas that she feared the worst: "I have the foreboding that we will pay for this with our lives."[37]

In addition to the bitter divisions within the Convention, the international situation had intensified. When Britain, Holland, and Spain recalled their ambassadors following the king's execution, the Convention declared war on them in February and March. General Dumouriez, a Girondin, lost to the Austrian forces in March, after which he deserted to their side. As denunciations increased between the factions, in April the Convention formed the Committee of Public Safety to serve as the executive. Finally, on 15 April, a deputation from the Paris sections demanded that twenty-two Girondin deputies be removed from the Convention. When the Girondin deputies voted against the Committee of Public Safety's price controls (Law of the Maximum), they further angered the Parisians, who had already turned against them.[38]

Parisians feared a federalist revolt led by Girondin supporters from Bordeaux, Caen, Lyon, and Marseille. They feared not only for their own safety but also for the loss of national unity. As a result, on 30 May 1793, anti-Girondin riots erupted in Paris, and by 2 June the Convention had expelled the Girondin deputies. Jérôme Pétion, who had earlier served as mayor of Paris, described their expulsion in dramatic terms: "Everything announced a grand catastrophe. The clouds surrounded our heads and the storm was ready to break."[39] Representatives of the radical Paris sections called for the impeachment of twenty-four Girondin deputies, and on 2 June the Convention, surrounded by armed men, had little choice but to give in to their demands. Some of the Girondin deputies had already fled from Paris, and others under house arrest also would attempt to escape in the days ahead.

It is not surprising then, given the tumultuous events of 1792 and 1793, that many of those who felt threatened should wish to leave France as quickly as possible. With little or no time to weigh their options, these involuntary émigrés fled before they faced almost certain arrest. Having no idea of what awaited them, they sought refuge wherever they could, many choosing the United States and sailing on the first available ship. These émigrés were largely composed of reform-minded members of the nobility and upper middle class, idealists and patriotic supporters of the revolution until the radicals took control of it. Making their temporary homes in the eastern cities of the United States, they attempted, with varying degrees of success, to make the best of the situation, some even enjoying the opportunity to lead an entirely different kind of life.

Perhaps the best known of these émigrés, due to their own writings and subsequent books about them, are Charles-Maurice de Talleyrand and Madame de la Tour du Pin. Talleyrand, the former bishop of Autun and a deputy in the Constituent Assembly, sailed to the United States from England, where he had gone on a diplomatic mission in 1792. The war between France and England and the passage of the Alien Bill necessitated his departure from England in March 1794. He arrived in Philadelphia in the early spring, and there he would join a small group of French refugees who had arrived earlier.

Talleyrand's rented house was located near the bookshop of Moreau de Saint-Méry, an émigré friend from the early days of the Constituent Assembly. The bookshop served as a genial meeting place for the French émigrés in Philadelphia, a place where they could gather in the evenings to sip Madiera wine and exchange stories about the revolution.

During the two and a half years that he spent in Philadelphia, Talleyrand befriended Alexander Hamilton, secretary of the Treasury, whom he greatly admired for his financial acumen. He also traveled to Maine and upper New York and engaged in land speculation, but he was more at home in cities. For this seasoned aristocrat, the United States lacked the style and refinement he had so enjoyed in France, and he was anxious to return home. Although he himself was greatly concerned with improving his own fortune, he found the Americans' obsession with money crude. In 1796 Talleyrand was able to leave the United States and return to France, where he would become minister of foreign relations for the new government of the Directory.[40] He would go on to serve later under the

First Empire of Napoleon and then again during the Bourbon Restoration, dying in 1832 after an extremely varied and influential life.

If Talleyrand had found the United States decidedly not to his taste, Madame de la Tour du Pin would enjoy a very different experience. Her journal covering the years from 1778 to 1816 contains many interesting and revealing descriptions of the two years that she and her family lived in New York State.[41] Henriette Lucie Dillon, married to the Marquis de la Tour du Pin, had served as one of Marie Antoinette's ladies-in-waiting before the revolution. Both her family and that of her husband enjoyed close connections with the French monarchy. Her father, Arthur Dillon, had served as governor of Tobago and became a deputy to the Constituent Assembly from Martinique; he was also a royalist supporter of the Girondin faction. In addition, her husband had been involved with others who had tried to save Louis XVI's life.

After the opening of the Estates General, Madame de la Tour du Pin had written perceptively about the situation in France, noting the general opinion that the Estates General would provide the reforms so badly needed by France. However, she also observed that there seemed to be no real concern about any inherent dangers, and wrote, "We were laughing and dancing our way to the precipice." That precipice arrived soon enough. Facing arrest in March 1793, the marquis and his family left Paris and fled to Bordeaux before he was forced to go into hiding. Fortunately, Madame de la Tour du Pin managed, through influential friends, to obtain passports for the United States, and the family was able to escape. Settling first in Albany, New York, they then bought a farm between Troy and Schenectady, where they would live for two years. According to her journal, Madame de la Tour du Pin lived contentedly as a "farmer's wife," cooking, washing clothes, and managing the slaves; obviously, she was living as a prosperous farmer's wife. Her husband, meanwhile, supervised and worked on the farm. Altogether, save for the death of their young daughter from yellow fever, their life in the United States, surrounded by natural beauty and friendly neighbors, was a beneficial experience. With some regret, they returned to France in May 1796. Many years later, in 1820, Madame de la Tour du Pin would write the journal that would make her famous.[42]

Other French émigrés during this period, while not as well known as Talleyrand or Madame de la Tour du Pin, also contributed in various ways to the exile experience in the United States. Méderic-Louis-Elie Moreau de Saint-Méry, a writer from a wealthy family in Martinique and a former member of the Constituent Assembly, left France in 1794. After passing his first few months in New York, he had moved on to Philadelphia, where he established a bookshop and a printing press. His bookshop reportedly resembled an enlightened French salon, which attracted a clientele limited to "nobles and outstanding educated commoners," and many of the regulars had served in the Constituent Assembly. They had been moderates, but after the monarchy fell in August 1792, moderation had become suspect, subject to interrogation and arrest. Moreau de Saint-Méry's bookshop, in effect, existed as "a small piece of the Republic of Letters in exile," surely a comforting venue for those who were far from home.[43]

Coming as he did from a family involved in the colonial judiciary, Moreau de Saint-Méry had conducted extensive research in the area of colonial administration. Therefore, during his four years in the United States, he finished writing and published two books, *Description de la Partie Espagnole de Saint-Domingue* and *Description de la Partie Française de Saint-Domingue*. In addition, during his exile he kept a diary titled *Voyages*, which provided an excellent contemporary account of French émigré life in the United States.[44] In 1798 Moreau de Saint-Méry returned to France, where he once again served in the government. He died in 1819.

Among those who gathered at Moreau de Saint-Méry's bookshop in Philadelphia were Louis-Marie Vicomte de Noailles, Omer Antoine Talon, Bon Albert Brois de Beaumetz, and the Duc de La Rochefoucauld-Liancourt. Both Noailles and Talon had arrived in the United States in May 1793. Noailles, like his future brother-in-law Lafayette, had fought in the American Revolution. From an ancient noble family, he had been elected to the Estates General in 1789, and later he had endorsed the abolition of feudal privileges. He served briefly in the French army, but in May 1792 he decided to resign due to the lack of discipline and proper military conduct. An idealist who had supported the early aims of the revolution, Noailles soon became disillusioned and decided to leave for the United States. It turned out that his decision to leave France in the spring of 1793 saved him from the fate suffered by his family: both his father and mother, as well as his wife, her mother, and her grandmother, were guillotined. Noailles, unlike his friends, did not return to France; instead, in 1803 he went to Saint-Domingue on business. There, along with others, he worked unsuccessfully to retain French control of the colony. Although he managed to escape on a boat, he was injured in a naval skirmish with the English. He later died in Cuba from the wounds he had suffered.[45]

Omer Talon, who had arrived at the same time as Noailles, hailed from a distinguished robe family and had served as a judge at the Châtelet before the revolution. He came late to the National Assembly, arriving in December 1789 when he replaced another deputy, the Comte de Montboissier. A known royalist primarily interested in judicial matters, Talon soon resigned from the assembly. He was implicated in the king's flight to Varennes and his name had been found on documents in the king' secret iron safe. Fearing arrest, Talon lost no time in getting out of France, going first to England before sailing to the United States, where he remained until after the Terror. Talon died in 1811 on the island of St.

Marguerite, where he had been deported following his implication in a royalist conspiracy.[46]

In 1794, Beaumetz and Liancourt joined the French émigrés in Philadelphia. Beaumetz, who had arrived in April, was from a judicial family in Arras, and he had served as a deputy for the nobility of Artois in the National Assembly. Beaumetz championed civil equality and individual freedom, and he worked to reform the penal system. He opposed punishment for émigrés and, along with other moderates, pushed for a general amnesty. Rather than remain in France and face arrest, he decided to leave for England; later, with Talleyrand, he had sailed to the United States. Beaumetz married an American widow, and in 1796 he traveled to India, where he planned to sell "American lands to the wealthy merchants of the East Indies." Upon his arrival in India, however, he discovered that another U.S. agent, Robert Morris, had already succeeded in carrying out his plan. Beaumetz died in India in 1800.[47]

Better known than either Beaumetz or Talon, the Duc de la Rochefoucauld-Liancourt arrived in Philadelphia in November 1794. In addition to having served as a lieutenant-general in the army, he was also an honorary member of the Academy of Science and "a somewhat philosophical economist" interested in modern agricultural pursuits. He became a deputy for the nobility of Clermont at the Estates General in 1789, later becoming one of the nobles who chose to join with the Third Estate. He was also one of the first nobles to purchase nationalized church property. Liancourt, who had accompanied Louis XVI from Versailles to Paris in October 1789, favored the constitution of 1791 and stood by the king in June 1792. After the fall of the monarchy in August, Liancourt lost his command in the army. Like so many others, he left France for England, sailed to the United States, and settled in Philadelphia. In 1796 he returned to France, where he resumed his work promoting agricultural and educational reforms. Liancourt died in 1827.[48]

As illustrated by the example of Moreau de Saint-Méry's Philadelphia bookshop coterie of temporary exilés, family and friendship networks helped to ease the transition from the familiar to the foreign. Most of those who left France between 1792 and 1794 had little time to do advance planning or to gather sufficient funds. Thus, they depended on those who could assist them without bothersome questions or fatal delays. Madame de la Tour du Pin relied on her friendship with Theresa Cabarrus (and Cabarrus's influence with Jean Tallien, the representative-on-mission in Bordeaux) to obtain passports for herself and her family.

Those in financial need frequently depended on their social networks to repay debts, borrow money, or even obtain funds for investment purposes. In addition, the wealthier exiles also assisted their political allies, as Talleyrand did with the Marquis de la Tour de Pin. In the early summer of 1795, he offered to loan the marquis twenty to twenty-five thousand francs, payable through his "banker-friend in Philadelphia." Later,

Talleyrand also was willing to loan Moreau de Saint-Méry sufficient funds to return to France. Earlier during his stay in Philadelphia, Saint-Méry had benefited from the generosity of his friends Cazenove and the Baron de la Roche.[49]

The Atlantic ports of New York, Philadelphia, Wilmington, and Norfolk were the most popular destinations for those émigrés who left France or Saint-Domingue in the 1790s. The fact that they were able to find not only material assistance but also emotional support through their already established social networks helped to ease the exile experience. That is not to say, however, that these French émigrés did not deeply regret their sudden dislocations. While they had surely saved their lives by fleeing, they could not escape the pain of separation from families and friends, or the shock of hearing news about their executions in France.

NOTES

1. See Theodore Thomas Belote, "The Scioto Speculation and the French Settlement of Gallipolis: A Study in Ohio Valley History," in *University Studies*, Series II, Vol. III, No. 3 (Cincinnati: University of Cincinnati Press, September–October 1907): 5–82.

2. Jocelyne Moreau-Zanelli, *Gallipolis: Histoire d'un Mirage Américain au XVIII Siècle* (Paris: L'Harmattan, 2000), 99–100, 103–4.

3. Moreau-Zanelli, *Gallipolis*, 105, 141–46; Belote, "The Scioto Speculation," 33.

4. *Papiers d'Eprémesnil*, Archives Nationales 158 AP, carton 12. The Duc d'Eprémesnil (1764–1794) was a conseiller of the Parlement of Paris and a noble deputy to the Constituent Assembly.

5. *Papiers d'Eprémesnil*.

6. Moreau-Zanelli, *Gallipolis*, 137–38, 147.

7. *Vente la Compagnie du Scioto*, Archives Nationales, Minutier Central, Etude V, 819–20; Etude XIII, 460, 468; Etude XX, 742.

8. Moreau-Zanelli, *Gallipolis*, Table des Ventes, 427–36.

9. Belote, "The Scioto Speculation," 45–47; Moreau-Zanelli, *Gallipolis*, 262–74.

10. Theodore Thomas Belote, ed., "Selections from the Gallipolis Papers," in *Quarterly Publication of the Historical and Philosophical Society of Ohio*, Volumes I–III (1906–1908): 80–82; Belote, "The Scioto Speculation," 47–49.

11. Belote, "The Scioto Speculation," 49.

12. Belote, "The Scioto Speculation," 49–52.

13. Belote, "The Scioto Speculation," 52.

14. Belote, "The Scioto Speculation," 52–53.

15. Belote, "The Scioto Speculation," 54; Moreau-Zanelli, *Gallipolis*, 345–47.

16. Moreau-Zanelli, *Gallipolis*, 346–47.

17. Belote, "The Scioto Speculation," 54–55

18. Moreau-Zanelli, *Gallipolis*, 358–63.

19. Belote, "The Scioto Speculation," 56; George W. Knepper, *Ohio and Its People* (Kent, Ohio: Kent State University Press, 1989), 69.

20. Belote, "The Scioto Speculation," 63–65; Moreau-Zanelli, *Gallipolis*, 333–37.

21. Moreau-Zanelli, *Gallipolis*, 338–39.

22. Knepper, *Ohio and Its People*, 64–65; Moreau-Zanelli, *Gallipolis*, 341–42.

23. Moreau-Zanelli, *Gallipolis*, 342–43, 355; *Gallipolis Papers*, III: C, 33–67, Cincinnati Historical Society, Cincinnati, Ohio.

24. Moreau-Zanelli, *Gallipolis*, 344, quoting from Albert de Lezay-Marnésia's *Mes Souvenirs à Mes Enfants*.

25. Moreau-Zanelli, *Gallipolis*, 366–69.

26. Belote, "The Scioto Speculation," 57.

27. Belote, "The Scioto Speculation," 57–59; Moreau-Zanelli, *Gallipolis*, 376–80.

28. Belote, "The Scioto Speculation," 59.

29. Francis S. Childs, *French Refugee Life in the United States: An American Chapter of the French Revolution* (Baltimore, Md.: Johns Hopkins University Press, 1940), 68–69.

30. Moreau-Zanelli, *Gallipolis*, 403–4. Lezay-Marnésia's project is not to be confused with the later more successful project of Asylum, organized by the émigrés Noailles and Talon and backed financially by Robert Morris and John Nicholson.

31. Moreau-Zanelli, *Gallipolis*, 405, 409. By 1798, the settlement had attracted 383 settlers. The land was transferred to North Louisiana in 1803, following the American purchase of Louisiana from France.

32. Moreau-Zanelli, *Gallipolis*, 405, #59.

33. Moreau-Zanelli, *Gallipolis*, 388–91.

34. Childs, *French Refugee Life in the United States*, 26–27, 34, 70.

35. P.-J.-B. Buchez and P. C. Roux, eds., *Histoire parlementaire de la Revolution française depuis 1789 jusqu'à l'Empire* (Paris: Paulin, 1833–1838), XIX: 410–12.

36. Owen Connelly, *French Revolution/Napoleonic Era* (New York: Holt, Rinehart and Winston, 1979), 129–30. For a detailed treatment, see David P. Jordan, *The King's Trial: Louis XVI vs. the French Revolution* (Berkeley: University of California Press, 1979, 2004).

37. Cl. Perroud, ed., *Correspondance, Lettres de Mme. Roland* (Paris: Imprimerie Nationale, 1900–1902), II: 457.

38. Connelly, *French Revolution*, 131–33; M. J. Sydenham, *The Girondins* (London: University of London, Athlone Press, 1961), 162–66.

39. Jérôme Pétion, *Mémoires de Jérôme Pétion, député à l'Assemblée Constituante, ensuite Maire de Paris et enfin député à la Convention Nationale, composé après Le 31 Mai 1793*, N. A. F. 1730, 83 (Paris: Bibliothèque Nationale, Dept. des Manuscrits).

40. Childs, *French Refugee Life in the United States*, 36; David Lawday, *Napoleon's Master: A Life of Prince Talleyrand* (New York: St. Martin's Press, 2007), 76–87.

41. Mme. La Marquise de la Tour du Pin, *Journal d'une Femme de Cinquante Ans, 1778–1815*, 2 vols. (Paris, 1903, 1920).

42. Childs, *French Refugee Life in the United States*, 24–27; Caroline Moorehead, *Dancing to the Precipice: Lucie de la Tour du Pin and the French Revolution* (London: Chatto & Windus, 2009), 95.

43. Doina Pasca Harsanyi, *Lessons from America: Liberal French Nobles in Exile, 1793–1798* (University Park: Pennsylvania State University Press, 2010), 1–2.

44. Childs, *French Refugee Life in America*, 33–35.

45. Harsanyi, *Lessons from America*, 33–34, 102–5; Childs, *French Refugee Life in America*, 31–32, 70–71.

During his exile in the United States, Noailles also was responsible for planning the settlement of Asylum in 1795, and he owned nineteen thousand acres out of the total of one million acres that the Asylum Land Company bought in the Susquehanna Valley. Managed by Talon, this settlement for French refugees from the Terror lasted until 1803, at which time the refugees went home and the Asylum Land Co. was dissolved.

46. Childs, *French Refugee Life in America*, 33; Harsanyi, *Lessons from America*, 36, 113.

47. Childs, *French Refugee Life in America*, 36–37; Harsanyi, *Lessons from America*, 34–35, 114.

48. Childs, *French Refugee Life in America*, 30–31; Harsanyi, *Lessons from America*, 27–30, 112.

49. R. Darrell Meadows, "Engineering Exile: Social Networks and the French Atlantic Community, 1789–1809" (81), *French Historical Studies* 23, no. 1 (Winter 2000): 67–102.

FOUR

Artists and Writers

Those who had chosen to remain in France or were unable to leave dealt with the rush of events and the changes in their lives as best they could. Some tried to keep out of sight or even went into hiding, while others made a show of their newly republican sentiments. Artists and writers, whose works had resulted in their public recognition, often found it difficult to strike the correct balance between creativity and patriotism.

Of the prominent women artists during the revolutionary period, only Elisabeth Vigée-LeBrun had chosen to emigrate. Adélaide Labille-Guiard, often seen by contemporaries as Vigée-LeBrun's rival, was one of the four women artists who had been accepted into the Académie Royale before it was abolished in the 1790s. Like Vigée-LeBrun, Labille-Guiard painted portraits, attempted history paintings, and attracted important clients. Their lives, however, as well as their painting styles and political sentiments, were markedly different. Labille had married Louis-Nicolas Guiard, a financial clerk, but they separated in 1779, after which she married François André Vincent, her teacher, but she continued to sign her name as Labille (femme) Guiard. While Vigée-LeBrun's paintings were often described as soft and feminine, Labille-Guiard's were judged to be more realistic and masculine. It was Labille-Guiard who had strongly opposed the "artificial barriers to the fulfillment of women's potential" and had worked to improve the status for women artists.[1] Enjoying a reputation as an excellent teacher, her paintings were exhibited alongside those of Vigée-LeBrun and Jacques-Louis David. One critic even praised her 1785 Salon painting, "Portrait de Madame Labille-Guiard and Her Pupils," as being of such high quality that it must surely have been painted by a man.[2]

Although Labille-Guiard had painted portraits of Louis XVI's aunts, she did not share Vigée-LeBrun's monarchist sentiments and actively

51

supported the revolution. In 1791 she exhibited fourteen portraits of deputies of the National Assembly.[3] Her portrait of Robespierre helped her to attract new and important clients, but even with her artistic success, she suffered some anxiety due to the loss of former patrons and friends, through either emigration or execution. It was the loss of one of her most important paintings, however, that dealt her a blow from which she never recovered.

In 1793 the revolutionary government ordered Labille-Guiard to destroy a large painting on which she had labored for two and a half years. The partially completed "Réception d'un Chevalier de l'ordre Saint-Lazare par Monsieur, Grand Maître d'ordre" had been commissioned in 1788 by the king's brother for 30,000 livres. Labille-Guiard had hoped that this monumental creation would lead to her receiving the coveted title of "Peintre d'Histoire" in the Académie Royale. Unfortunately, by 1793, the king's brother, the Comte de Provence, had already emigrated and the Académie had been abolished.

The government ordered the painting to be destroyed, because it glorified the monarchy, and it was unlikely that payment for it would ever be received. In addition, one could hardly afford to portray any aspect of the monarchy in a favorable light in 1793. Very reluctantly, therefore, Labille-Guiard obeyed the order to give up not only the partially completed portrait but also all of the studies related to it, after which the painting was burned.[4]

For the artist, the destruction of a creation on which she had lavished great care not surprisingly led to emotional anguish and disappointment. Labille-Guiard never again attempted to create such a demanding work, and she sent few offerings to subsequent Salons. Her health declined and she died in 1803. Ironically, she had been the only one of the four prominent women artists who had actively favored the revolution, and (artistically, at least) she had become one of its victims.[5]

The two other successful women artists of the period, Anne Vallayer-Coster and Marguerite Gérard, managed to flourish during the revolution and also avoided incurring the displeasure of the government. Vallayer-Coster, the daughter of the king's goldsmith and a member of the Académie Royale, was esteemed for her still-life paintings as well as for her portraits. She had attracted powerful supporters, including Denis Diderot and even Marie Antoinette, who arranged for her to have a studio in the Louvre's Grande Galerie in 1779. Although Vallayer-Coster made no secret of her Bourbon sympathies, she and her husband, the wealthy lawyer Jean Pierre Silvestre Coster, remained in Paris during the revolution. Apparently the nonpolitical nature of her paintings—primarily flowers, soup tureens, vegetables, and fish—and the fact that most of her work appeared between 1769 and 1787, did not arouse the hostility of the government. In contrast, Vigée-LeBrun's well-publicized friendship with the queen and her many acclaimed portraits of royalty and aristocrats had resulted in celebrity status, thus making her an object of particular distaste for the government. Vallayer-Coster had painted only one portrait of Marie Antoinette in 1780, but it has since disappeared. She exhibited few works at the Salons between 1793 and 1810, choosing in her later years to create tapestry designs for the Gobelins factory. Vallayer-Coster died in 1818.[6]

Marguerite Gérard, unlike Vigée-LeBrun, Labille-Guiard, and Vallayer-Coster, did not enjoy membership in the Académie Royale, since the four places reserved for women artists had already been filled by 1783. Nevertheless, she managed to achieve a significant reputation as a genre painter in the neo-Dutch style and her work was appreciated by other artists, including David, and art dealers, notably Jean-Baptiste Pierre Le-Brun, who showed her works in his gallery. Gérard's paintings, mostly small generic domestic scenes, did not portray well-known figures or aristocrats; therefore, they posed no dangers politically.

Gérard had moved from Grasse to Paris in 1775, and there she joined the household of her older sister Marie-Anne, who had married the well-established artist Jean-Honoré Fragonard in 1768. Gérard would live with the Fragonards in their apartment in the Louvre for thirty years.

By 1789 Gérard's work already had received considerable attention from the sales of engravings of her genre scenes as well as from the presence of her paintings in private collections. It is probable that she had seen many Dutch genre scenes at LeBrun's gallery, where she first exhibited her own work publicly in 1789. She must also have been familiar with LeBrun's book of engravings of such paintings, *Galerie des Peintres Flamands, Hollandais et Allemands*, published in 1792–1796.[7]

LeBrun, an outspoken champion of the seventeenth-century Dutch genre painters, also was cognizant of their commercial value, especially following the collapse of the Ancien Régime. His interest in contemporary French artists who shared his views prompted him to offer exhibition space at his gallery, and he bought at least one of Gérard's paintings, "La Fuite," before his 1789 exhibition.[8] Gérard's work was often described as being in the "Metsu manner"—that is, highly finished interior scenes reminiscent of the Dutch artist Gabriel Metsu. Her paintings, however, could be purchased for considerably less than those by the Dutch master.

Gérard's life and career differed greatly from that of her illustrious contemporary Vigée-LeBrun, although they shared the same circle of artist friends, notably Robert, Vernet, David, and others. While Gérard came from a humbler background and only began painting after moving to Paris and living with the Fragonards, Vigée-LeBrun had been instructed from childhood by her artist father, Louis Vigée, who taught at the Académie de Saint-Luc. Their painting styles and subject matter also differed markedly, as did their political persuasions. Unlike as their lives were, however, both artists possessed sufficient managerial skills to ensure that they would enjoy financial security throughout their lives. If Vigée-LeBrun is better known today than other woman artists of the period, it is partly owing to her colorful memoirs, published in 1835–1837. She also outlived most of her contemporaries, dying only in 1842. Vigée-LeBrun had accumulated most of her wealth through the sales of her work, while Gérard, who continued to exhibit at the Salon through 1824, had made a number of successful real estate investments over the years. She died in 1837.[9]

It is entirely plausible that LeBrun, the great-nephew of the Sun King's painter Charles LeBrun, and married to an artist/celebrity, found the role of mentor to younger artists a satisfying one. In addition, the situation of being married to an émigré caused him great difficulty; consequently, he sometimes felt snubbed and unappreciated for his professional opinions. His situation would soon improve, however, thanks to the influence of Jacques-Louis David, who would make it possible for LeBrun to play an important role in the transformation of the Louvre from a royal to a national museum.

As early as October 1792, LeBrun had warned Minister of the Interior Roland about the dangers of poor conservation methods and had asked to be hired as a restoration expert.[10] Even with David's support, however, LeBrun's requests were denied at that time. David, for his part, worked actively to discredit the Commission des Monuments and the Museum Commission, and to centralize every facet of arts administration. The Commission des Monuments, which had been responsible since 1790 for safeguarding art from the royal and ecclesiastical collections (as well as art from émigré collections since 1792), was replaced by the Commission Temporaire des Arts in August 1793.[11]

LeBrun, who had publicly attacked both Roland and the Museum Commission, urged the appointment of better-qualified commissioners and suggested that an eighteen- to twenty-member department of the arts be created as soon as possible, and he cited David's support of his position. LeBrun had justified his criticism of Roland and the Museum Commission by declaring, "I love the arts and the truth . . . a Republican has only his country before his eyes."[12] The hostility between LeBrun and Roland only increased after Roland disputed LeBrun's assertions in an open letter dated 16 January 1793 to the newspapers.[13] Roland would be replaced by Dominique Garat, another Girondin, in January 1793; Garat served in that position until his resignation the following August.

David, elected to the National Convention in 1792, continued to push for LeBrun, along with Jean-Michel Picault, to be hired as commissioner-experts at the national museum. Finally, in August 1793, they were both hired, and LeBrun was able to compile the catalog for the grand opening of the Museum Français, as it was then known, on 10 August. His position would also give him an influential voice in future evaluation and acquisition decisions, which would increase markedly in the next ten years with the confiscations of art treasures from throughout Europe.[14]

When the national museum opened to the public on 10 August 1793, it became a highly visible symbol of the new republic. As a public institution, it could serve to educate those who visited the galleries as well as continue to appeal to informed amateurs. Opening as it did during a chaotic period in the revolution, however, presented some problems. In a letter dated 2 August to Garat, LeBrun warned that not only were pictures still arriving at the museum but the workers also needed to be paid.[15] Despite his misgivings, the Museum Français opened as planned, featuring 537 oil paintings, most of which came from the royal collection. Other paintings exhibited had been the property of the now suppressed churches and monasteries. Works from the Académie, abolished by a decree of 8 August, as well as from émigré collections, were not shown at the opening, although they would appear later at the museum. The grand opening on 10 August was considered a major accomplishment, and one that was generally appreciated by the public, who now could visit three days a week free of charge. The other days were reserved for artists and special guests.[16]

The date of 10 August had also been chosen for the Festival of National Unity, a spectacle intended to celebrate the glorious change from a monarchy to a republic. Approximately two hundred thousand citizens participated in a grand procession, viewing as they walked various revolutionary images that had been designed by David. Visual representations of the Ancien Régime, such as the fleur-de-lys, had been replaced by more appropriate republican ones, like the fasces. An effective bit of propaganda, the staging of the Festival of National Unity on the same day as the opening of the Museum Français sent a strong visual message of national purpose. Furthermore, the government had been willing to spend 1,200,000 livres to ensure that its message was communicated clearly, not only in Paris but also elsewhere, through written reports and letters.[17]

LeBrun, meanwhile, found himself in an advantageous position. The decisive battle of Fleurus on 26 June 1794, in the war with Austria, had led to the French occupation of Belgium and to government authorization of the confiscation of art works. The Committee of Public Instruction had recommended that several artists and scholars be dispatched to accompany and advise the French army on matters of confiscation, and on 8 July, LeBrun became one of four men appointed for that purpose. They were directed to prepare instructions for generals in the field on the proper removal and conservation procedures. The choice of LeBrun had been mandated by his extensive knowledge of Flemish, Dutch, and German art, as exemplified by his three-volume *Galerie des peintres Flamands, Hollandais et Allemands*.[18] By September 1794, between six and seven hundred paintings filled the Museum Français depot, the confiscated art works further complicating the problems associated with selection, reparation, and arrangement in the Grand Gallery.[19]

LeBrun, an active participant in artistic matters of national importance, played a pivotal role at this time—speaking out, writing letters, and publishing pamphlets—in addition to his work at the national museum. Archival documents offer proof of his meticulous inventories as well as his complaints and requests for funds.[20] His ideas were presented clearly in a thirty-page pamphlet, "Quelques Idées sur la Disposition, l'Arrangement et la Décoration du Muséum National," which was distributed free of charge at his gallery.[21] In the conclusion LeBrun suggested that a scholarly catalog would help "shed light" among those who were worthy of appreciating "the benevolence of our legislators."[22]

Until Dominique Vivant-Denon took charge of the museum in 1803, when it became the Musée Napoleon, LeBrun used his knowledge as a connoisseur and art dealer to influence not only the selection and arrangement of art works but also which methods of restoration to employ. It is highly unlikely that he would have been able to hold such an important position had he not divorced his wife when he did, in addition to making good use of his connections with David, a deputy allied with the radical faction in the National Convention. David did sign some arrest warrants for artists when he served on the Committee of Public Safety, but he did not send any of his fellow artists to the guillotine, and he himself served time in prison after the Terror ended in 1794.[23]

While David's alliance with the radical faction had worked in LeBrun's favor, it produced just the opposite effect for his good friend, the poet André Chénier. David and Chénier had met in the 1780s, when both frequented the homes of the wealthy Trudeau brothers in the Place Royale. Charles-Louis Trudaine de Montigny and Charles-Michel Trudaine de Sablière, sons of an intendant of finances, had known Chénier since their school days at the Collège de Navarre, and, like their father, they were patrons of the arts. They had taken a special interest in David, from whom they commissioned the "Three Horaces" and "The Death of Socrates." Reports circulated that Chénier had suggested the best pose for Socrates to take in the famous painting. Chénier and David also belonged to the Société de 1789, a liberal group of 660 members, most of whom could be described as political moderates. The group included Lafayette, Bailly, Mirabeau, La Rochefoucauld, Condorcet, Roederer, Chamfort, and the Trudaines; however, many members who had also belonged to the Jacobin Club left the Société in 1791 and joined the Feuillants, a club for constitutional monarchists.[24]

Chénier's essay, in August 1790, for the *Journal de la Société de 1789,* "Avis au Peuple Français sur les veritables ennemis," praised the revolution but warned against the power of the people and their "eruptions."[25] It is safe to say that Chénier did not favor the increasing radicalism of the revolution and would have preferred a constitutional monarchy to a republic. That he made no secret of his opinions on the matter would lead to his eventual prosecution by the Jacobin government.

Chénier also wrote a long political poem about David's famous painting, "Le Serment du Jeu de Paume." One of only two of Chénier's poems published in his lifetime, the twenty-four-page work was dedicated to "Louis David, Peintre," and published in March 1791. The publisher, Bleuet, was known as "a center of right-wing propaganda," an indication of the direction in which Chénier was moving. The first part of the poem paid tribute to artistic freedom, a matter on which both Chénier and David had long agreed, but toward the end of the poem Chénier warned about the dangers of careless orators who gave voice to slanders and conspiracies.[26]

David and Chénier remained friends until at least April 1792. Earlier in March David had agreed to create a painting of Louis XVI showing the constitution to his son, an appropriate work meant to pay tribute to the new constitutional monarchy. The radical press wasted no time in attacking David for accepting such a commission, at which point Chénier wrote an article in response to David's critics. An admirer of the English form of government, Chénier favored the stability that he thought would result from a constitutional monarchy in France, and he stated as much in his article in the *Supplement au Journal de Paris*.

Although David had made some preparatory sketches for the painting, he decided not to complete the project, perhaps a signal that he was moving further left politically. It is difficult to determine whether David chose to move in that direction as a result of the radicals' criticism of the proposed painting or because he actually endorsed the radical position. It is entirely possible that David, as with LeBrun, merely chose to pursue a policy of survival. His friend Chénier, an outspoken idealist, obviously had chosen to follow a more dangerous path.

David, meanwhile, decided to join Chénier's brother Marie-Joseph and the composer François-Joseph Gossec in the preparation of a festival honoring the Chateauvieux regiment, a group of enlisted men who had rebelled against their officers in August 1790 and consequently received harsh punishment. The treatment of the Swiss regiment had attracted extensive attention through debates in the press, with arguments for and against the regiment's rehabilitation. David's participation in the proposed festival only served to increase the division between André Chénier and his brother. Their falling out had resulted from André's attack on the radicals, titled "On the Cause of the Disorders that trouble France and impede the Establishment of Liberty." Appearing on 26 February 1792, only two weeks after Marie-Joseph's play, *Caius Gracchus*, had opened, André's polemic stirred his brother to defend himself and claim that he did not share André's opinions.[27] Marie-Joseph did not want the government to associate André's opinions with his own, a wise move on his part, but one that was sure to antagonize his brother. Marie-Joseph also publicized his membership in the Jacobins, the club that had been attacked by his brother. The matter of the festival to honor the Chateauvieux regiment only exacerbated the political differences between the brothers and finally ended the friendship between André Chénier and David.[28]

On 24 March, David, Marie-Joseph Chénier, Collot d'Herbois, Jean-Lambert Tallien, and Théroigne de Méricourt presented a petition for official support of the festival to the Commune. Following its acceptance by the Commune, André Chénier argued against it in an article in the *Journal de Paris* and, in addition, he denounced the Jacobin sponsors of the festival. As might be expected, the radical press responded forcefully, accusing Chénier of being "a false and perfidious writer, and a sterile poet." In turn, on 10 April, André Chénier accused Collot d'Herbois of stupidity and "cowardly slander." Despite the back-and-forth, however, the festival honoring the Swiss regiment was held on 15 April, featuring songs and decorations by Marie-Joseph Chénier and David.[29]

André Chénier continued to criticize the Jacobins until the events of 10 August 1792, after which he fled from Paris and went into hiding. He collaborated with the Feuillants and occupied himself with political journalism in the *Journal de Paris*. While he despised the Jacobins, Chénier also had little patience with the more moderate Girondins, who were pushing France into a war with other European monarchies. In addition to his articles, Chénier composed a controversial political poem, the "Hymne aux Suisses de Chateauvieux," published on 15 April 1792 in the *Journal de Paris*. The poem, a sort of parody of the numerous ceremonial odes and hymns that accompanied celebrations during the revolution, employed a new verse form consisting of alternate alexandrines and octosyllabics, which attracted much attention to its author.[30]

Chénier's poetry had evolved from his early neo-classical works of "purely intellectual activity into a poetry of commitment . . . a bridge between Racine and Hugo." Although he was little appreciated during his own lifetime, he became more popular when his poetry was published in 1819. Chénier was greatly admired by the Romantics, who perceived him as a symbol of the poet as hero, and his legend has continued to attract both readers and operagoers ever since.[31] His life and death inspired Umberto Giordano's opera, *Andrea Chénier*, first performed in 1896, as well as Charles-Louis Muller's dramatic painting of 1850, titled "The Last Roll Call of the Victims of the Terror." Several other lesser-known plays and novels were also inspired by the life and tragic death of André Chénier.[32]

André Chénier was arrested on 7 March 1794, almost by chance, and sent to Saint-Lazare, a former monastery that had become a prison known as the Maison Lazare. The charges brought against him by the Revolutionary Tribunal actually applied to his brother, Sauveur Chénier, who also had been imprisoned at Saint-Lazare. Despite his protests, however, the thirty-one-year-old poet was judged guilty and sentenced to death on 25 July 1794 (7 Thermidor). If only his execution date had been set a bit later, Chénier would have survived. As it turned out, he was not as fortunate as his former good friend David, an ally of Robespierre's who chose not to attend the National Convention on 9 Thermidor due to illness.[33]

Reports circulated that Chénier and his friend, the poet Jean-Antoine Roucher, recited the verses of Racine as they were transported to their executions at the Place du Trone, now called the Place de la Nation. Following their executions, the bodies were placed in a nearby field behind the Picpus convent. Chénier and the others executed that day were thrown into a common grave, which holds the remains of all those who perished between 14 June and 27 July 1793. A commemorative plaque on the wall of the "Fosse Commune" at Picpus Cemetery honors the fallen poet. It reads, "André de Chénier, fils de la Grèce et de la France, 1762–1794. Servit Les Muses Aima La Sagesse Mourut pour la Vérité."

There is little doubt that Chénier felt keenly the loss of his future as poet, for he had just begun to develop an individual, mature style when his voice was silenced. A strong believer in his own particular genius, Chénier had moved from the artistic self-centeredness of youth to the beginnings of a strongly felt concern for the needs of others. His last poems, written in prison, expressed his feelings of loss, as when he wrote, "Toi, Vertu, pleure si je meurs," and his epitaph included the words "Tu dors, o mon génie! Un Dieu t'appelle, accours. Éveille-toi."[34]

Had Chénier been more politically astute or if his timing had been better, it is likely that he could have survived. His stubborn idealism had prevented him from keeping his views to himself or pretending to agree with either the Jacobins or the Girondins. Still, had he remained outside of Paris until the Terror had passed rather than returning from Versailles in 1793, his chances would have been decidedly better. Chénier had left Paris in 1792 and hidden in various nearby locations including Marly, Louveciennes, and Saint-Germain-en-Laye. He had also visited Rouen, where many other moderates, royalists, and independents had gone in 1792, as well as Le Havre. His brother Constantine was planning to leave for Alicante, where he had been assigned as consul, and the opportunity existed at that time for André Chénier to sail from France. A letter to his father indicated that he had already obtained the false papers needed for travel.[35] Yet, for unknown reasons, after settling in Versailles in 1793, Chénier chose to return to Paris. Perhaps he thought that his father, a section representative, could protect him or that his estranged brother Marie-Joseph might be helpful. Whatever Chénier's reasoning, the decision to return to Paris during the Terror proved to be not only unwise but also fatal.

As with André Chénier, the journalist and aphorist Sébastien-Roch Nicolas Chamfort had also evolved from youthful self-regard to a greater concern for others. Unlike Chénier, however, Chamfort moved in the same circles as the leading Girondins such as Roland. Born illegitimately in 1740 in Clermont-Ferrand, Chamfort had made good use of his natural intelligence and wit to gain a scholarship for study in Paris, after which his literary skills and opportunism had enabled him to attract aristocratic patrons including the Comte de Vaudreuil. His plays were performed at the Comédie Française in 1764 and 1776, and he was elected to the Académie Française in 1781.

A success under the Ancien Régime, Chamfort nevertheless became an early supporter of the revolution, favoring political reforms and a constitution. He joined the Club of Thirty, along with his good friend Mirabeau and others including Condorcet, Talleyrand, and Sieyès, and it was Chamfort who suggested the title for Sieyès's famous pamphlet, "What Is The Third Estate?" He also joined the Société de 1789.[36] In addition to writing articles for *Le Mercure*, Chamfort wrote some of the commentaries for the *Tableaux Historiques*, a series of popular prints about revolutionary events, and collaborated with his friend Pierre-Louis Ginguené on *La feuille villageoise*, a newspaper created to increase peasant support for the revolution.[37]

Chamfort counted the Rolands, both the interior minister and his wife, as good friends, and he often attended the weekly meetings held in their Paris apartment, where the Girondins discussed political matters. Even so, Chamfort required much urging before he accepted Roland's offer to serve as the co-director of the new national library. Finally, in August 1792, Roland appointed Chamfort and Jean-Louis Carra, a Girondin and the co-founder of *Annales Patriotiques*, to the post, which required good patriots as well as able administrators. The co-directors of the formerly royal library were expected to transform it into a national institution, but they were paid little to carry out their duties. Not only were they directed to expand the library's hours of operation, but they were also told to fire any personnel who appeared insufficiently patriotic.[38]

As interior minister, Roland took seriously his responsibility to protect the national heritage of art works in the Museum Français and the manuscripts, books, prints, and coins in the Bibliothèque Nationale. Since many of the items once had belonged to the monarchy, Roland feared (with good reason) that they might be destroyed or stolen by overly enthusiastic patriots. In an effort to prevent such actions, Roland, in a letter dated 18 December 1792, instructed Chamfort to transport the royal materials to the Tuileries for inventory, after which he was to place them in a "special room" in the library. Chamfort would understand the unstated message in such instructions, since he had previously participated in secret propaganda activities for Roland.[39]

The royal materials destined for the "special room" in the library included the personal libraries of Louis XVI and of Talleyrand, who had emigrated in 1794; the Prince de Condé's medals; seventeen thousand gold objects from the church of Sainte-Geneviève in Paris; and items from the royal tombs at Saint-Denis. Objects and books from the Royal Depository and the Tuileries Palace and valuable manuscripts from the Sorbonne and Saint-Germain-des-Près, in addition to the genealogies of aristocrats and other papers and books that were considered "useless" by the revolutionary government, were also saved. [40]

The more difficult part of Chamfort's work involved the termination of some of the experienced librarians, who were to be replaced by more obviously patriotic but not necessarily more capable employees. In a typically brusque letter to Hugues-Adrien Joly, who had worked for many years in the Department of Prints and Engravings, Chamfort directed him to turn in his keys immediately, collect his belongings, and leave the library. Joly's son Jean-Adrien (known as Joly fils) also was asked to leave, a decision that Chamfort would soon regret because Joly's replacement, Tobiésen-Duby, would cause him no end of trouble. [41]

Despite the loss of experienced librarians, Roland specified that "the library will be open every day to the public," instead of several hours, three days a week, to specialists. Thus, the co-directors were expected to provide more and better service with fewer librarians, even as the budget allocated for library operations continued to shrink. [42]

Along with the other Girondin leaders, by 1793 Roland faced increasing opposition from the radical faction in the government. The Girondins had been discredited by their more moderate position during the king's trial, and Roland, in particular, had been criticized by the Museum Commission, notably by LeBrun and David, who were eager to appoint new members. Roland resigned as interior minister on 23 January 1793, but during his brief tenure he had managed to legislate protective measures for France's historical treasures as well as to contribute his efforts toward the transition of both the museum and the library from royal to national institutions. His successful work during this tumultuous period of the revolution has not always been properly acknowledged. [43]

By the late spring of 1793, the Girondin deputies had been expelled from the National Convention. Many of them, like Roland, had fled into hiding, but twenty-nine others, including Manon Roland and Carra, had been arrested. Carra's arrest meant that Chamfort had to assume all of the directorial duties himself. Known as a friend of the Girondins, he found that he was under attack as well; in his newspaper, *L'Ami du Peuple*, Marat had already accused him of being too bourgeois. But like André Chénier, Chamfort did not keep his thoughts to himself. He cheered openly at the news that Marat had been assassinated by Charlotte Corday on 13 July and praised her courage in ridding Paris of "King Marat." [44] Tobiésen-Duby wasted no time in denouncing Chamfort's remarks in a letter dated 21 July to the Committee of Public Safety. He referred to Chamfort and several other library employees as "sly aristocrats" and "false patriots" who contributed to undermining the revolution, while he, Tobiésen-Duby, was an "ardent patriot." [45]

Perhaps Chamfort was not too surprised when, at dawn on 2 September, he and several of his colleagues (Barthélemy, Desaulnays, and Capperonnier) were arrested and taken to the Madelonettes prison. With its unhygienic conditions and bad food, this former convent had a reputation as one of the worst prisons in Paris. Chamfort at that time was suffering from poor health and the prison experience horrified him; he vowed that he would never allow himself to be imprisoned again. [46] During their two days at the Madelonettes, however, Chamfort and the other prisoners did enjoy an impromptu performance by some of the actors from the Comédie Française, who had also been imprisoned. They performed a play by François de Neufchâteau, *Pamela ou la vertu récompensée*, which had been deemed reactionary by the government. [47]

After their release from prison, Chamfort and his colleagues were kept under watch by a guard housed near the library. In addition, Tobiésen-Duby continued to attack Chamfort in the press, referring to him as an "aristocrat." In a public letter dated 8 December 1793, Chamfort denied the accusation, suggesting instead that Tobiésen-Duby was motivated by envy and actually wanted to become the director of the library. On 9 September, unable to carry out his duties properly, Chamfort decided to resign and concentrate on defending himself and trying to help the imprisoned Carra. [48]

He did not, however, remain quiet; rather, he continued to speak openly, even around his guard. This guard once mentioned that the theaters in Paris suffered from poor attendance. In reply, the aphorist Chamfort declared, "Tragedy no longer has the same effect once it roams the streets." [49] During this period the theater was intended to serve as an instructional sphere, with particular attention to egalitarianism among the audience. For example, the opening night at the Théatre National in August 1793 had featured *La Journée de Marathon*, "a musical allegory of France's war effort set in ancient Greece," a suitably patriotic choice. The press, however, chose to focus on the absence of boxes near the stage, which formerly had been reserved for aristocrats. [50]

Chamfort had hired a lawyer to defend Carra but to no avail, for Carra and twenty-one other proscribed Girondin deputies were executed in October 1793. In characteristic fashion, Chamfort observed, "The revolution is a lost dog that no one dares to collar." When he was notified on 15 November that he must return to prison, Chamfort, pleading the need to pack, went into his dressing room, closed the door, and attempted suicide. He had aimed the pistol at his forehead but ended up smashing the upper part of his nose and his right eye; he subsequently tried to cut his throat and wrists with a razor. Despite his determined efforts, Chamfort had not succeeded in killing himself, but he was so severely wounded that he could not be taken to prison.

Chamfort managed to partially recover from his wounds, and he even regained his liberty since he was no longer considered a threat. In January 1794 the Committee of Public Safety awarded him and eleven of his former library colleagues 2,000 livres annually as "pensioners" of the Republic.[51] In a last literary effort, Chamfort joined his friend Pierre-Louis Ginguené, who would serve as director of public instruction from 1795 to 1798, and several journalists in the creation of a new publication, *La Décade Philosophique*. Backed by Madame Helvétius and edited by Ginguené, the review sought to strengthen the ideals of the Enlightenment.[52] A few months later Chamfort fell ill, probably as a result of the improper drainage of one of his self-inflicted wounds, and he died on 13 April 1974 in his small apartment near the national library.

His loyal friend Ginguené wrote about this period, "The Terror was so widespread that it represented an act of courage just to accompany Chamfort to his final resting place." Indeed, only a few of his friends, including Ginguené, Sieyès, and Van Praet from the library, accompanied Chamfort's body to the cemetery of Les Innocents.[53]

Ginguené saved what he could of Chamfort's literary output, publishing four volumes of his work in 1795.[54] Other manuscripts apparently had been stolen before they could be retrieved from Chamfort's apartment, and their location remains a mystery. The works that did survive to be published—aphorisms, thoughts, and anecdotes—sufficed to ensure Chamfort's reputation as a keen observer of his society. These observations, "the products of the perfected civilization," as their author had ironically titled them, had been written over a period of many years on small squares of paper and deposited into boxes in his bedroom. His friends assumed that Chamfort had intended to write a history of manners, but had never found the time. Nevertheless, it is these trenchant observations that have made Chamfort's ideas known to later generations, rather than his early plays or journalism or his work as co-director of the national library.[55] Had he not tried to avoid prison by attempting suicide, Chamfort might have lived to write a great deal more. Like Chénier, however, he also needed to express himself, to make his opinions known, even at the risk of arrest and death.

The director's position at the national library was filled by Jean-Baptiste Lefebvre de Villebrune, a scholar-librarian who had been responsible for denouncing some of those arrested or executed during the Terror. Unpopular with the remaining thirty-three staff members, he was replaced late in 1795 by Jean-Augustin Capperonnier, who reorganized the library administration, worked to preserve the collections, and oversaw the compilation of inventories of confiscated books and manuscripts.

Even Jacques-Louis David, a staunch ally of Robespierre and his associates, did not entirely escape punishment. Following the executions of 9 Thermidor, David was arrested on 2 August and imprisoned until 26 December. He was arrested again, as were former members of the Committee of Public Safety, in May 1795, victims of the Thermidorian Reaction. David defended his own actions during the Terror, explaining that he had only marched "in the revolutionary line traced by the dominant opinion of the period." If he had done anything wrong, he protested that it was due to "the excess of my love for la patrie," and he declared that his intentions had always been just.[56] Following his release from prison, David resumed his artistic career, and as Napoleon's court painter he would be responsible for creating some of the most dramatic images of the emperor.

David, like LeBrun, had managed to navigate the uncertain currents of the revolution. Had he been present at the meeting of the National Convention when his associates were arrested, it is unlikely that he would have been so fortunate. His supposed illness on that particular day was fortuitous. As in the case of André Chénier and others to be discussed in a later chapter, timing could make all the difference between survival and death.

NOTES

1. Ann S. Harris and Linda Nochlin, *Women Artists 1550–1950* exhibition catalogue, Los Angeles Museum of Art (New York: Alfred A. Knopf, 1976), 185–86.

2. Pierre Rosenberg, "Introduction," *French Painting 1774–1830: The Age of Revolution* exhibition catalogue (Detroit, Mich.: Wayne State University, 1975), 517–18; see also *Collection Deloynes*, Salon criticism (1783–1824), vol. XIV, no. 344, 662–63 (Paris: Bibliothèque Nationale, Departement des Estampes).

3. Colin B. Bailey, "Collectors of French Painting and the French Revolution," in *1789: French Art during the Revolution*, exhibition catalogue, ed. Alan Wintermute (New York: Colnaghi, 1989), 244.

4. Bailey, "Collectors of French Painting," in *1789: French Art during the Revolution*, 244.

5. Anne-Marie Passez, *Adélaide Labille-Guiard 1749–1803* (Paris: Arts et métiers graphiques, 1973), 56–57. This is the definitive monograph on Adélaide Labille-Guiard.

6. The standard source for Vallayer-Coster is Marianne Rolland-Michel's *Anne Vallayer-Coster* (Paris: Comptoir international du livre, 1970). See also Danielle Rice, "Women and the Visual Arts," in *French Women and the Age of Enlightenment*, ed. Samia I. Spencer (Bloomington: Indiana University Press, 1984), 248; and Harris and Nochlin, *Women Artists 1550–1950*, 179–80.

7. Sally Wells-Robertson, *Marguerite Gérard: 1761–1837*, 4 vols. (doctoral dissertation, New York University, 1978), vol. I, part 1: 235, 258, 112; Jean-Baptiste Pierre LeBrun, *Galerie des peintres Flamands, Hollandais et Allemands*, 3 vols. (Paris, 1792–1796) (Paris: Bibliothèque Doucet, Fol. F212).

8. Wells-Robertson, *Marguerite Gérard*, vol. II, part 2: 951.

9. See Wells-Robertson, *Marguerite Gérard*, vol. I, part 1: 257, 291, and 274; Elisabeth Vigée-LeBrun, *Souvenirs*, 3 vols. (Paris: Librairie de H. Fournier, 1835–1837). The English translation of *Souvenirs*, by Sian Evans, is titled *The Memoirs of Elisabeth Vigée-LeBrun* (Bloomington: Indiana University Press, 1989).

10. Letters from LeBrun to the Minister of the Interior, F17 1058, dossier 1, Archives Nationales, Paris.

11. Bailey, "Collectors of French Painting," in *1789: French Art during the Revolution*, 14.

12. LeBrun, *Réflexions sur le Muséum National* (Paris, 1792), 19, 20.

13. Edouard Pommier, *Édition et Postface de Réflexions sur le Muséum National, 14 janvier 1793*, by Jean-Baptiste Pierre LeBrun (Paris: Réunion des Musées Nationaux, 1992), 79.

14. Andrew McClellan, *Inventing the Louvre: Art, Politics, and the Origins of the Modern Museum in Eighteenth-Century Paris* (New York: Cambridge University Press, 1994), 105.

15. Letter dated 2 August 1793 from LeBrun to Citizen Minister, F17 1057, dossier 1, Archives Nationales, Paris.

16. Cecil Gould, *Trophy of Conquest: The Musée Napoléon and the Creation of the Louvre* (London: Faber and Faber, 1965), 26–29.

17. Warren Roberts, Jacques-Louis David, and Jean-Louis Prieur, *Revolutionary Artists: The Public, the Populace, and Images of the French Revolution* (Albany: State University of New York Press, 2000), 296; McClellan, *Inventing the Louvre*, 97–98.

18. LeBrun, *Galerie des peintres*, Fol. F212. The others chosen to advise the army were the Abbé Gregoire, A. C. Besson, and Varon.

19. McClellan, *Inventing the Louvre*, 114.

20. See F17, 1056–1059 and F21, 570–571, Archives Nationales. LeBrun was always short of funds due to a gambling habit, and he continued to ask his wife for money, even when she went into exile.

21. Jean-Baptiste Pierre LeBrun, *Quelques Idées sur la Disposition, l'Arrangement et la Décoration du Muséum National* (Paris, 1794) (Paris: Bibliothèque Doucet 8 F990).

22. LeBrun, *Quelques Idées*, 28. For a detailed discussion of this topic, see Bette W. Oliver, *From Royal to National: The Louvre Museum and the Bibliothèque Nationale* (Lanham, Md.: Lexington Books, 2007).

23. Simon Schama, *Citizens: A Chronicle of the French Revolution* (New York: Alfred A. Knopf, 1989), 846; Bailey, *1789: French Art during the Revolution*, 212.

24. Francis Scarfe, *André Chénier: His Life and Work, 1762–1794* (Oxford: Clarendon Press, 1965), 58–59; Roberts, *Revolutionary Artists*, 237–38.

25. Scarfe, *André Chénier*, 221–23.

26. Scarfe, *André Chénier*, 229; Roberts, *Revolutionary Artists*, 240–41.

27. Roberts, *Revolutionary Artists*, 250–51.

28. Roberts, *Revolutionary Artists*, 251.

29. Roberts, *Revolutionary Artists*, 251–52.

30. Scarfe, *André Chénier*, 253, 271. Scarfe provides a detailed analysis of Chénier's poetic works.

31. Scarfe, *André Chénier*, 366. See also the collection of Chénier's manuscripts in the Bibliothèque Nationale, Dept. des Manuscrits, NAF 6848-6852.

32. The painting "The Last Roll Call of the Victims of the Terror" is at the University of Notre Dame, Smite Museum of Art.

33. Roberts, *Revolutionary Artists*, 258.

34. Scarfe, *André Chénier*, 353, 355–56, 364. A total of 1,306 men and women were executed between 14 June and 27 July 1793.

35. Scarfe, *André Chénier*, 281–82.

36. Claude Arnaud, *Chamfort, A Biography*, trans. Deke Dusinberre (Chicago: University of Chicago Press, 1992), 154, 183; Kenneth Margerison, *Pamphlets and Public Opinion: The Campaign for a Union of Orders in the Early French Revolution* (West Lafayette, Ind.: Purdue University Press, 1998), 58.

37. Roberts, *Revolutionary Artists*, 60–63.

38. "Correspondance relative à l'administration et au personnel de la Bibliothèque royale II, 1781–1792," Archive 47 (Paris: Bibliothèque Nationale, Dept. des Manuscrits); "Dépenses de la Bibliothèque nationale, 1791 — An X, états et traitements," F17 3439, Archives Nationales.

39. *Papiers Roland* (1732–1793), N. A. F. 9532, 321 (Paris: Bibliothèque Nationale, Dept. des Manuscrits); Arnaud, *Chamfort*, 222–23.

40. "Dépenses de la Bibliothèque nationale, 1791—An X," F17, 3439, Archives Nationales; *Papiers de van Praet* (Paris: Bibliothèque Nationale, Dept. des Manuscrits); Arnaud, *Chamfort*, 224.

41. See Archive 47, Bibliothèque Nationale, and F17 3439, Archives Nationales.

42. Letter dated 19 August 1792 from Interior Minister Roland to Chamfort. T1458, Archives Nationales.

43. *Papiers Roland*, N. A. F. 9532, 334. For a detailed treatment of the transition from royal to national institutions, see Oliver, *From Royal to National*.

44. Arnaud, *Chamfort*, 239–40.

45. Simone Balayé, *La Bibliothèque Nationale des Origines à 1800* (Geneva: Librairie Droz, 1988), 363–64.

46. *Papiers de van Praet*; *Dossier Chamfort*, F7 4638, Archives Nationales; Simone Balayé, "La Bibliothèque Nationale pendant la Révolution," in *Histoire des Bibliothèques Françaises: Les Bibliothèques de la Révolution et du XIX Siècle, 1789–1914*, vol. 3, ed. Dominique Varry (Paris: Promodis-Éditions de la Cercle de la Librairie, 1991), 75.

47. Alain Sanders, *Petit Chronique de la Grande Terreur* (Maule: Éditions de Présent, 1989), 39–41.

48. Balayé, *La Bibliothèque Nationale des Origines à 1800*, 366–67; Arnaud, *Chamfort*, 246–47.

49. Arnaud, *Chamfort*, 248: *Oeuvres complètes de Chamfort* (Paris: Auguis, 1824–1825), 5: 340–41.

50. Arnaud, *Chamfort*, 248–49; James H. Johnson, *Listening in Paris: A Cultural History* (Berkeley: University of California Press, 1995), 99–101.

51. Balayé, *La Bibliothèque Nationale des Origines à 1800*, 368–69.

52. Arnaud, *Chamfort*, 254.

53. Pierre-Louis Ginguené, preface to Chamfort's *Caractères et Anecdotes* (Paris: Crès, 1924), lviii; *Collection Ginguené*, N. A. F. 9192, 9193, 9195 (Paris: Bibliothèque Nationale, Dept. des Manuscrits).

54. Pierre-Louis Ginguené, ed., *Oeuvres de Chamfort*, 4 vols. (Paris, 1795).

55. Arnaud, *Chamfort*, 256–58; Sébastien Chamfort, *Products of the Perfected Civilization*, trans. and with an introduction by W. S. Merwin (San Francisco: North Point Press, 1984).

56. Roberts, *Revolutionary Artists*, 313.

FIVE

Rule by Terror

The autumn of 1793 was witness not only to the executions of Marie Antoinette, twenty-one former Girondin deputies, and Madame Roland, but also to that of the Gregorian (Christian) calendar. Time itself had been officially altered and reordered. By decrees of 5 October and 24 November, the National Convention established the Revolutionary Calendar, which contained twelve months of thirty days each and three ten-day weeks in each month. Meant to do away with Christian days of worship, the calendar eliminated Sundays, saint's days, Easter, Christmas, and all church holidays. Sundays were replaced by Décadi, or tenth days. Even the names of the months were changed to reflect the weather of the seasons. The five days remaining at the end of each year were labeled *sans-culottides*, set aside to celebrate revolutionary virtues. As if these changes were not sufficient to cause discomfort and confusion among the populace, the new calendar became retroactive; therefore, 1792–1793 became Year I of the Republic, 1793–1794, Year II, and so on. This unsettling distortion of time continued until it was abolished under the First Empire in 1806.[1]

Despite the radical reordering of time, the conversion of churches to temples of reason, and the staging of spectacles such as the Festival of Liberty and Reason on 10 November 1793, the ordinary people of France remained attached to their familiar forms of worship and commemoration of the dead as well as to their priests as mediators between this world and the next. By forcing the clergy to take an oath to support the revolutionary government, the legislators had managed to alienate many parishioners, who found themselves cut off from their usual sources of spiritual comfort.[2]

The violence and insecurity of the autumn of 1793 had only been exacerbated by the government's efforts to enforce reason during an extraordinary period of accelerated change. Many of those under attack by the government earlier in 1793, including some of the expelled Girondin deputies, had fled from Paris while it was still possible. Others who chose to remain in Paris faced imprisonment and execution. Following his resignation in January, Jean Roland had gone into hiding in the Rouen area in March. His wife Manon, however, did not join him, even though she knew that she was in danger. Earlier, in December 1792, she had been ordered to appear before the National Convention, where she was accused of involvement in a royalist conspiracy. While the charge was later dropped, both she and her husband remained under suspicion by the government. Although it cannot be proved, she may have remained in Paris because the Girondin deputy François Buzot was still serving in the National Convention during the early months of 1793. They had formed a romantic attachment, said to be platonic, and the dutiful and virtuous Manon had admitted as much to her husband.

Coincident with the anti-Girondin riots and the expulsion of the deputies, Manon Roland was arrested again on 1 June and taken to the Abbaye prison. Perhaps in a spirit of shared martyrdom with other victims of the Terror, she wrote from her prison cell, "I absolutely dedicated myself to my destiny, whatever it may be."[3] During her next five months in prison, Manon would pass the time by writing her memoirs and by corresponding with Buzot, who had escaped from Paris to Caen in early June along with some of the other expelled deputies. It was possible for prisoners to send and receive letters by means of visitors, who agreed to smuggle them into and out of the various prisons. Although none of Buzot's letters to her have survived, several of Manon's letters to him, written in June, July, and August 1793, are preserved in the Bibliothèque Nationale. In one of her letters dated 22 June, Manon wrote that she had been greatly relieved to hear from him and to learn that he was safe. She assured him that, in her ten-foot square cell, she was leading "the life here that I led in my study at home," adding that she enjoyed the freedom of her thoughts "behind bars and bolted doors." She also asked Buzot not to attempt anything rash for her sake and warned him that the mail could be intercepted if sent through official channels.[4]

Manon Roland had always enjoyed expressing her thoughts in written form, and in prison she had sufficient uninterrupted time to undertake an extended work titled *Appel à l'impartiale postérité*. The first part of her memoir concentrated on the revolutionary period and the injustices perpetrated by the radical government, while the second part examined her childhood and youth in a surprisingly frank manner. Since she was a very disciplined and conscientious person who took pleasure in writing, it is probable that Manon was able to momentarily escape her prison walls in the process. At the very least, her prison memoir ensured that she would be remembered by later generations.[5]

It is ironic that earlier in her life Manon had disdained women of letters who flaunted their intellectual achievements. She had felt then that one's personal thoughts should be confined to private notebooks. In a letter to her friend Bosc in 1783, she had written, "No matter what their [women's] facility may be in some respects, they should never show their learning or talents in public."[6] The revolution had put an end to such traditional ideas, however, and Manon, who had even helped her husband compose his reports as interior minister, felt free enough in prison to finally express her private thoughts.

When Manon was released from the Abbaye prison on 24 June, she dared to hope that she might be allowed to live quietly and safely. Almost as soon as she had reached her home, however, a deputation from the Committee of Public Safety arrived and charged her with alleged conspiracy against the revolution and complicity with her husband and the other Girondins. This time she was taken to Sainte-Pélagie prison. There she resumed her prison routine of reading, writing, and visiting with the occasional friend. Her former cell at the Abbaye prison, meanwhile, would hold two other well-known occupants: the Girondin leader Jacques Brissot, and then Marat's assassin Charlotte Corday.[7]

Fearing that Buzot and his Girondin associates might try to rescue her, in a letter of 6 July Manon urged Buzot to be calm, and she claimed that she had expected to be moved to "this second prison," which was not true. She assured him that she would have a public hearing before the Revolutionary Tribunal and expressed confidence that she would be exonerated. In an effort to cheer and encourage Buzot, in her letters she continually expressed an optimism that she did not feel. She also wrote that she "shared his danger" and hopes for progress within the departments, a reference to a planned federalist revolt against the government in Paris.[8] Buzot would receive his last letter from Manon, dated 31 August, after he and his friends had fled from Caen to Brittany. Although the letter had been disguised and addressed to the husband of Manon's childhood friend Sophie Cannet, the closing words left no doubt of both her precarious situation and her love for Buzot: "Goodbye. Oh! How you are loved!"[9]

When she heard about the guilty verdict for the twenty-one imprisoned Girondins who had appeared before the Revolutionary Tribunal on 24 October, Manon realized that there was little chance for her own survival. The deputies had not been allowed to defend their actions, nor would she. Manon was transferred to the Conciergerie prison, where all condemned prisoners were sent, on 31 October. Under questioning, she refused to implicate those who had visited her home, and she insisted that she had only served as her husband's secretary rather than as part of a "secret bureau." She appeared before the Revolutionary Tribunal on 8 November, fully prepared to present an eloquent defense of her actions, but she was denied that opportunity. Based on the discovery of her correspondence with the Girondin fugitives in Caen, Manon was accused of conspiracy against the republic and sentenced to die within twenty-four hours.[10] As she approached the platform on which the guillotine stood, a dignified and composed Manon Roland turned to gaze upon the large statue of Liberty nearby. Never at a loss for words, she now spoke those that would be quoted by so many others from that day on: "O Liberty, what crimes are committed in thy name!"[11]

On 10 November when Jean Roland heard the news of his wife's execution, he walked a few miles outside the city of Rouen and shot himself. He had lost everything that mattered to him except his daughter Eudora, who had been placed in the care of the family of the deputy Creuzé-Latouche by Manon. Roland had escaped from Paris in time to save himself from the authorities, but apparently his survival had become meaningless without his wife. For her part, Manon probably could have survived if she had chosen to leave Paris earlier, yet for her own reasons she had remained and risked arrest. To all appearances, she had accepted her martyrdom willingly.

News of the death of Manon Roland reached Buzot, now in hiding in St. Emilion near Bordeaux, by 15 November. He had feared such an outcome and was overcome with grief, as a letter to an old friend in Evreux, Jérôme Le Tellier, made clear. "*She* is no more, *she* is no more, my friend. The scoundrels have murdered her," he wrote. "Consider if there is anything left for me to regret on earth."[12] A fugitive in the republic that he had helped to create, Buzot recalled that at one time he and Manon had considered fleeing to Switzerland, or even to America, but they had decided that it was their duty to remain in France. In his memoir he wrote that France was still dear to him, despite the cruel treatment he had received, and he would miss it should he leave never to return.[13]

Buzot and Brissot had been among the first of the expelled deputies to flee from Paris the previous June. While Buzot and several of his friends had managed to flee to Caen, then to Brittany, and finally to St. Emilion between June and November, Brissot had not even made it as far as Caen.[14] Reaching Versailles by 5 June, Brissot had been joined by Joseph Souque, a friend from the Jacobin Club in Paris. Before setting off for Caen, however, Brissot decided to visit his hometown of Chartres, where he expected to receive a warm welcome. In his memoir he expressed disappointment at the cool reception from his old friends in Chartres, who feared to associate with an expelled deputy.[15]

The detour to Chartres had slowed their progress, but Brissot and Souque headed first to Orléans, which turned out to be unsafe, and then to Moulins. They were required to stop and show their passports at every village along the way, which increased the possibility that they might be recognized. Souque reasoned that it would be wise to arrive in Moulins very early in the morning when the guards were apt to be less attentive, but Brissot, pleading exhaustion, insisted on stopping for the night at an inn near Nevers. Much like Louis XVI during his flight to Varennes, a few hours' delay would make all the difference in the outcome of the journey. As Brissot would write later in his memoir, "Minutes are as centuries in revolutions."

By the time they reached Moulins at mid-day on 10 June, the numerous guards were fully awake and suspicious of the new arrivals. Brissot waited in the carriage while Souque took their false passports for inspection. One police officer questioned Brissot's Swiss passport, which identified him as a merchant named Alexandre Ramus; consequently, Brissot had to leave the carriage and appear in person. The officer was not convinced, however, and he chose to refer the matter to the mayor and the council of the Department of the Allier. Since Brissot carried neither trunks nor papers with him, he could not convince the council that he really was a Swiss merchant. As a result, both he and Souque were arrested.[16]

When he appeared before the Comité de Surveillance, Brissot admitted his true identity, and he requested that his case be referred to the National Convention. While they waited for a decision from Paris, Brissot and Souque remained under arrest in Moulins; they were soon joined by Don José Marchena, a young Spaniard who had been exiled from his country for expressing revolutionary views. Marchena had come to Moulins expressly to stand with Brissot and share his misfortunes, because not long before, it had been Brissot who had brought him to Paris from Bayonne.[17]

On 19 June the authorities in Moulins were relieved to receive the decree from the National Convention ordering Brissot's transfer to Paris. The city square had filled with spectators that afternoon, some of them shouting, "To the guillotine!" By seven o'clock that night Brissot and his two friends were en route to Paris in three carriages, escorted by civil authorities and police officials. Hostile crowds met them in Montargis, and their carriages were marked with insulting caricatures. In his memoir Brissot recalled the incident: "Nothing could be more like a dance of cannibals around their victim attached to the fatal stake than the sight of those monsters announcing to me with a jubilant air the approaching guillotine." Rather than being afraid, however, Brissot wrote that he was "heartbroken" to think that he had sacrificed so much for men such as these.[18] On the morning of 22 June, the carriages reached Villejuif, one of the entries to Paris where the prisoners would be temporarily detained. Brissot had hoped to be placed under house arrest, but instead he was taken to the Abbaye prison, where he would remain until he was transferred to the Conciergerie in early October.

The case against Brissot and his fellow Girondins was presented in Saint-Just's report to the National Convention on 8 July. Brissot was singled out for special criticism by Saint-Just, who accused him of "intriguing both in internal and in foreign affairs, first to save the king, and then to reestablish royalty and to divide the Republic. . . . He used his influence against peace in October 1792, and besides, threatened the Convention with the arms of England and Spain; and to gain influence in America, had his brother-in-law appointed vice-consul-general at Philadelphia." Brissot also was accused of "conspiracy with Dumouriez in favor of royalty," and his wife was accused of being part of a conspiracy at Saint-Cloud, where "they planned the destruction of the Republic."[19]

On 28 July the National Convention passed a decree based on Saint-Just's report that named eighteen Girondin fugitives as traitors. Brissot, Deperret, and others were already in prison, while six others including Condorcet had been proscribed earlier.[20] Those named as traitors were condemned for their flight from Paris as well as their attempts to incite rebellion in the departments of Calvados, Eure, and Rhone et Loire. Even those who had not fled but had chosen to remain in Paris were perceived as accomplices of the fugitives.

While some of those same fugitives continued to seek safety outside of Paris, Brissot occupied his time in prison by preparing a written response to Saint-Just's accusations. He dismissed the charges of royalty and federalism as "contradictory," since each system excluded the possibility of the other. In addition, he noted that the counter-revolutionary movements within the departments had occurred but after the 2 June purge in the National Convention, not before.[21] Denying the charge of royalism, Brissot explained the Girondin preference for suspension rather than dethronement of Louis XVI as a means to avoid rule by regency. The Girondins had favored instead a total change in both the government and its personnel. Brissot claimed that he could not recall a request for humane treatment for the king after 10 August, but he defended such a request. "Would cruelty be a republican virtue?" he asked.[22]

Brissot declared that he was "profoundly republican," citing his words of 24 October 1792, which had held that three revolutions were necessary in France: "the first to reverse despotism, the second to put an end to royalty, the third to destroy anarchy. Anarchy, I repeat, is the most dangerous enemy of the republican government."[23] He had said as much earlier in 1791 in his book about his travels in America, when he had compared France unfavorably with America. "The habitual practice of reason produces . . . principled men," he had written, adding that in France he saw "only unstable, excitable persons who do good by impulse and in fits of enthusiasm, never as a result of reflection." Declaring that reflection is necessary at every stage for the revolution to succeed, he asked, "What can give better proof of the worth of a political system than its results?"[24]

Brissot denied that he had been "the author of this war [with Austria]"; rather, he wrote that the war had been the fault of the émigrés, the emperor, and the electors. He also denied playing any part in the invasion of Belgium or the war with England, writing that if Louis XVI's fate had been decided by a plebiscite, the European monarchies would not have recalled their ambassadors, a move that had set the stage for war. Regarding the appointment of his brother-in-law, François Dupont, to a post in Philadelphia, Brissot countered by declaring that Dupont was "a republican by principle," who had resided in the United States since 1789. Dupont had sailed to the United States at the same time, December 1788, that Brissot was returning to France after his American travels. Brissot also denied having anything to do with the Girondin ministry's decision to send Edmond Genet to the United States as a minister from France in February 1793. He explained that Genet's "merit" had recommended him for the post, and that he had already provided proof of his patriotism by serving as a diplomat at the Russian court.[25]

While Brissot's denials about being "the author of the war" seem a bit disingenuous considering his fervent pro-war articles in the *Patriote Français* during the period leading up to the war, his protestations about his wife's conspiratorial actions ring true. Following Brissot's flight from Paris in June, Félicité Brissot and their three children had sought seclusion by renting two rooms in the apartment of the concierge at Saint-Cloud. Félicité's actions had led to accusations by Brissot's captors that his wife, who was living in near poverty, was actually part of a salon conspiracy located in the former royal palace. After Brissot's arrest angry crowds had gathered outside of Félicité's apartment, making it necessary for her to seek refuge elsewhere. She and the children, however, soon were discovered and placed under arrest by the Committee of General Security of the municipality of Saint-Cloud. Brissot, meanwhile, had no knowledge of his family's difficult situation.[26]

Sitting in his cell in Paris, Brissot concentrated on finishing his written defense. After recapitulating his arguments about the charges made against him in the report of 8 July, he declared that he had served his country and the cause of liberty for the past four years. "Posterity will judge me," he wrote. Brissot also defended his friends Souque and Marchena as principled men, good patriots, and republicans.

Vehemently denying that he had amassed any "riches" during the revolution, Brissot pointed out that he and his family lived on the fourth floor of an "obscure apartment" on the rue de Grétry. His books were the only things of value in that apartment, he wrote, and they were valuable only to him. In addition, he explained that he still owed approximately 25,000 francs for debts incurred eight years ago, and as a result of his devotion to the work of the republic, his wife and children had suffered; they needed to depend on generous friends for help. His "perpetual sacrifice" for the public good had not resulted in their enlightenment, he lamented, and he was horrified by the corruption of those who had allowed it to happen. By 8 August Brissot had completed his detailed and eloquent defense. His closing words were characteristically idealistic and optimistic: "Innocence is in my heart, justice is in the people, sooner or later they will proclaim my innocence. I am awaiting therefore with tranquility their judgment and yours."[27]

While Brissot had been occupied with writing his response to Saint-Just, he also had been in communication with friends on the outside, and through them with Manon Roland after her move to the Sainte-Pélagie prison. The authorities had transferred her to prevent communication with Brissot, but the two still managed to communicate through their mutual friends—Mentelle, Bosc, and Champagneux. Apparently it was Manon who convinced Brissot to write his memoir while awaiting judgment in prison. Before he was sentenced, Brissot passed his memoir on to Mentelle, who in turn offered to send the manuscript to Manon. Fearing its "irreparable loss" or confiscation, however, she suggested that he send her a copy instead.[28]

Brissot continued to appeal to the Committee of Public Safety and to the National Convention, asking for a hearing and for permission to see his wife, her mother, and her sister. On 3 July the Committee of Public Safety allowed him to communicate with the latter two but not with Félicité, because they suspected both Brissot and his wife were involved in a conspiracy. Already in the Convention there had been demands for an immediate trial of Brissot by the Revolutionary Tribunal. For his part, Brissot protested vigorously the idea of his involvement in any kind of conspiracy: "Yes, I conspire with my triple locks and my triple bars! I conspire alone or with the philosophes of antiquity who teach me to bear the wrongs which I suffer for the cause of liberty, that cause of which I shall always be the apostle."[29]

On 27 July the National Convention had appointed Robespierre to the Committee of Public Safety and he quickly became its primary spokesman. Unlike Danton, the Committee's previous, more moderate leader, Robespierre was not inclined to share power with the Convention. He had little choice, however, about listening to the radicals in Paris, because he needed their support. Consequently, two radical members—Collot d'Herbois and Jean Nicolas Billaud-Varenne—were added to the Committee of Public Safety in September. Fearing that the Committee was the government's only defense against outright anarchy, the Convention went along with its recommendations for legislation. Following the murder of Marat earlier that July, Robespierre, in a speech at the Jacobin Club, had called for a "'Government of Terror', death to the enemies of the Republic, and a nation in arms." His words became law, as "the Convention dutifully voted terror to be the 'Order of the Day.'"[30]

Changes were not long in coming. The constitution of 1793, approved by the electors in August, was suspended by the National Convention, which also ordered the establishment of maximum prices on food and provided for minimum wages. In addition, the Committee of General Security, created in 1792, was revitalized by its zealous new leaders, André Amar and Marc Vadier, whose mission comprised rounding up all of the "traitors" within France. Once arrested, such "traitors" would be judged by the Revolutionary Tribunal, which was directed by the lawyer Fouquier-Tinville. Two of the four sections of the Revolutionary Tribunal were in session twenty-four hours a day, with ten to sixteen judges and sixty jurors assigned for each case. The sentences, from which appeals were not possible, were often severe and carried out immediately; those convicted had their property confiscated.[31] As an instrument of terror, the Revolutionary Tribunal exerted its intended effect on the populace, as they observed an increasing number of executions from October 1793 through June 1794.

The popular eighteenth-century composer André Grétry has described vividly the stark contrast between the spectacle of the guillotine at work and the ordinary pleasures of life. Writing about music, he had pointed out that the listener's sensibilities were moved by the contrasts within a composition. He then recounted how he had experienced one such contrast as he walked toward home one evening. Having just visited a lovely garden on the Champs-Elysées, where a magnificent lilac tree was in full bloom, Grétry wrote that he was walking near the Place de la Révolution. He passed some dancers and musicians enjoying themselves, and then he raised his eyes and saw at a distance the blade of the guillotine rising and falling, "twelve or fifteen times in succession. Country dances on one side of me, streams of blood flowing on the other, the scent of flowers, the gentle influence of spring, the last rays of the setting sun which would never rise again for those unhappy victims."[32] Such contrasting tableaux became all too common in Paris and elsewhere in France during the months of the Terror.

On 3 October, in order to hasten their trials, André Amar presented a general indictment against Brissot and the other accused Girondins. The indictment of forty-five counts echoed Saint-Just's earlier report, but it was longer and more comprehensive. Brissot was named once again as the leader of the Girondins and the one most suspected of conspiracy "against the liberty and safety of the French people." Brissot reacted to these charges in his usual fashion, writing a lengthy defense in which he made a determined effort to clear his name and to prove that he was and had always been a sincere patriot. As an example of his untiring work on behalf of France, he cited his journey to America, which had been undertaken "to learn how to bring about a like revolution in France," and how, after he returned to France, he had "embarked on the dangerous career of a journalist in order that he might daily combat the prejudices, the abuses of despotism, and aristocracy."[33] His words were actually a mixture of truth and wishful thinking: he had gone to America, on behalf of his friend Clavière, who had financed the trip, primarily to investigate investment, trade, and settlement opportunities; and while Brissot had always worked for reforms, he also had long been a journalist and undoubtedly enjoyed his position of influence as the editor of the *Patriote Français*.

Brissot's detailed written response, in which he refuted every charge made against him, ended abruptly, an indication that he was not given sufficient time to finish it before he went before the Revolutionary Tribunal. After a preliminary examination on 15 October, Brissot and the twenty other Girondins were called before the Tribunal on 24 October. Every witness called, either radicals or members of the Paris Commune, made hostile assertions without providing evidence.[34] As a result of some ad hoc legislation rushed through by Robespierre and Barrère, the report of the trial, in the Archives Nationales, presented only the brief responses of the accused. This legislation allowed the president of the court "to end proceedings as soon as the jury were sufficiently enlightened, and so to prevent speeches for the defense from being heard."[35]

There is some doubt regarding the accuracy of the records of the trial, since the brief procès-verbal in the Archives Nationales does not include the testimony. In addition, the reports in the *Moniteur* and the *Bulletin du tribunal révolutionnaire* were written using information from the enemies of the accused. Considering also that many of the charges were based on hearsay and that the witnesses were biased, the trial itself can be seen as a travesty of justice. According to Brissot's lawyer, Chaveau Delagarde, his client was not given an opportunity to present a final defense.[36]

The Revolutionary Tribunal announced on 30 October that no further evidence was required and declared that all of the accused were guilty. It had been assumed that the Girondins, supposedly a *parti*, had acted in unison against the policies of the government: "For the revolutionary, all opposition is necessarily counter-revolutionary, and preconcerted, and if all could be accused as conspirators, all could be convicted on a single capital charge." Even those Girondins who had chosen to remain in Paris were not excused from their associations with those who had fled in June.[37]

If contemporary reports are to be believed, to those sitting in the courtroom on the night of 30 October, the verdict of guilt with "punishment by death" brought forth exclamations of disbelief, shock, and innocence. According to one witness, Brissot was almost overcome with emotion. Camille Desmoulins supposedly blamed himself for his earlier denunciatory pamphlet, *Brissot dévoilé*, and cried out, "My God! I am sorry for you! This is a horrible day!" The condemned Valazé withdrew a dagger from beneath his coat and stabbed himself in the heart. Reportedly, the Girondin prisoners even threw *assignats* to observers in the courtroom, perhaps to precipitate a rescue effort. The crowded, torchlit courtroom presented a dramatic spectacle not likely to be forgotten in later descriptions of revolutionary events, some of which were undoubtedly exaggerated for effect.[38]

The prisoners passed their last night of life in the Conciergerie, where condemned prisoners waited to go to their executions. Now a national historic site in the heart of Paris, the former prison housed more than two thousand seven hundred persons during the Terror. Few details exist about the Girondins' last hours, but one witness wrote that they remained courageous as they spoke quietly among themselves, wrote last letters, and even sang. Although confessors were provided, Brissot did not make use of one, but he did assure his friends that he believed in an eternal life after death. He also managed to write letters to his family, knowing well that they would face further difficulties on his account. His poverty was so acute at this point that when he was transferred to the Conciergerie, he did not even have the thirty-three livres necessary for a bed and food. His friends paid the fee for him. [39]

Brissot's letter to his wife Félicité made clear his own perception of the situation. "I see, my dear Félicité, that my last hour has come," he wrote. "Perhaps I shall have the misfortune of not being able to see you again; yet I would give everything to be able to. If this happiness is refused, bear the blow with courage. You owe it to our children; watch over them; look out for them. Keep some of my notes to show them some day. They will say: 'This is the writing of a father who loved us, and better than us loved the public good, for he sacrificed himself and has been sacrificed for it. . . .' Adieu, my loved ones, wipe away your tears. Mine are wetting this paper. But our separation will not be eternal." [40]

Brissot had no way of knowing that on the day of his execution Félicité and her youngest child had been arrested and placed in La Force prison. There they would remain until 19 February 1794. During that terrible period, Félicité's mother, Madame Dupont, took care of the two older children and, following Félicité's release from prison, she continued to assist her and the children.

The condemned Girondin prisoners were placed in carts and escorted to the Place de la Révolution on 31 October. Legend has it that they joined in singing "La Marseillaise" as they were transported through the city on the way to the guillotine. Even those who had vilified them admitted that the former Girondin deputies presented a brave spectacle for the large crowds gathered to watch. According to police reports, Sillery was executed first and Brissot last, with the entire process taking only twenty-six minutes. It could only have been an added cruelty for the Girondin leader to be forced to watch the executions of his comrades. The twenty-one former deputies were subsequently buried at the cemetery of the Madeleine. [41]

As he had written earlier in his book about America, Brissot had suspected that his countrymen were not yet "mature enough for liberty, for a free man is a rational man." He had despaired at the small number of true patriots to be found, and noted, "Simple needs and tastes may indeed be the only sure signs and guarantees of patriotism. A man of few wants," he had written, "is not forced to sell himself. . . . To enslave a nation you do not always need a Bastille."[42]

From the autumn of 1793 through July 1794, twenty-six hundred persons would be guillotined in Paris, while as many as fifty thousand throughout France would be executed. Some would be shot and others drowned, as in Nantes, where prisoners were chained on barges, which then were sunk in an estuary of the Loire River. Eighty-five percent of those executed were neither nobles nor priests, but rather members of the Third Estate, such as the former Girondin deputies.[43]

NOTES

1. Owen Connelly, *French Revolution/Napoleonic Era* (New York: Holt, Rinehart and Winston, 1979), 159, 221. On 22 September 1792, the National Convention had ordered public documents to be dated from Year I of the Republic.

2. Joseph Clarke, *Commemorating the Dead in Revolutionary France: Revolution and Remembrance, 1789–1799* (Cambridge: Cambridge University Press, 2007), 86.

3. Cl. Perroud, ed., *Mémoires de Madame Roland* (Paris: Plon, 1905), I: 28.

4. *Correspondance 1793* (letters from Madame Roland to Buzot), N. A. F. 1730, 2–5 (Paris: Bibliothèque Nationale, Dept. des Manuscrits).

5. Gita May, *Madame Roland and the Age of Revolution* (New York: Columbia University Press, 1970), 264. Edited by Louis Bosc, Mme. Roland's memoir was published by Jean-Baptiste Louvet in Paris in 1795.

6. Cl. Perroud, ed., *Correspondance, Lettres de Mme. Roland* (Paris: Imprimerie Nationale, 1900–1902), I: 256–57.

7. May, *Madame Roland*, 271–72.

8. *Correspondance 1793*, N. A. F. 1730, 6–15.

9. *Papiers Roland* II, N. A. F. 9533, 222 (Paris: Bibliothèque Nationale, Dept. des Manuscrits).

10. May, *Madame Roland*, 282.

11. *Papiers Roland* II, N. A. F. 9533, 296.

12. *Mémoires de François-Nicolas-Louis Buzot*, N. A. F. 1730, 16 (Paris: Bibliothèque Nationale, Dept. des Manuscrits).

13. *Mémoires de Buzot*, N. A. F. 1730, 22–24.

14. For a detailed account of the Girondin fugitives in 1793–1794, see Bette W. Oliver, *Orphans on the Earth: Girondin Fugitives from the Terror, 1793–1794* (Lanham, Md.: Lexington Books, 2009).

15. Cl. Perroud, ed., *J.-P. Brissot, Mémoires 1754–1793* (Paris: Librairie Alphonse Picard & Fils, 1910), II: 216.

16. Perroud, ed., *J.-P. Brissot, Mémoires*, II: 221–22.

17. Perroud, ed., *J.-P. Brissot, Mémoires*, II: 225–26. Marchena regained his freedom in Paris and joined the other expelled Girondins in Caen. He was captured later in the Bordeaux area and imprisoned in Paris.

18. Perroud, ed., *J.-P. Brissot, Mémoires*, II: 226–28.

19. Eloise Ellery, *Brissot de Warville: A Study in the History of the French Revolution* (Houghton Mifflin, 1915; reprint, New York: Burt Franklin, 1970), 363–64. She cites the *Moniteur* of 18 and 19 July 1793.

20. M. J. Sydenham, *The Girondins* (London: University of London, Athlone Press, 1961), 217. The list of traitors included Buzot, Pétion, Gorsas, Barbaroux, Louvet, Guadet, Salle, Bergeoing, Chasset, Defermon, Kervélégan, Henri-Larivière, Chambon, Lidon, Valady, Rabaut Saint-Etienne, Lesage de L'Eure, and Lanjuinais.

21. Perroud, ed., *J.-P. Brissot, Mémoires*, II: 231–35.

22. Perroud, ed., *J.-P. Brissot, Mémoires*, II: 240; Ellery, *Brissot de Warville*, 365–66.

23. Perroud, ed., *J.-P. Brissot, Mémoires*, II: 241–42.

24. J.-P. Brissot de Warville, *New Travels in the United States of America*, 1788. Trans. Mara Soceanu Vamos and Durand Echeverria (Cambridge, Mass.: Belknap Press of Harvard University Press, 1964), 14–15.

25. Perroud, ed., *J.-P. Brissot, Mémoires*, II: 251–58; Ellery, *Brissot de Warville*, 366.

26. Perroud, ed., *J.-P. Brissot, Mémoires*, II: 259–61; Ellery, *Brissot de Warville*, 387, 403.

27. Perroud, ed. *J.-P. Brissot, Mémoires*, II: 262–71.

28. Ellery, *Brissot de Warville*, 367–68. For a detailed discussion of Brissot's memoir, see Cl. Perroud, "Étude Critique sur Les Mémoires de Brissot" in *J.-P. Brissot, Mémoires*, vii–xxviii.

29. Ellery, *Brissot de Warville*, 368–69.

30. Connelly, *French Revolution*, 135–36.

31. Connelly, *French Revolution*, 136–37.

32. Anselm Gerhard, *The Urbanization of Opera: Music Theater in Paris in the Nineteenth Century*, trans. Mary Whittall (Chicago/London: University of Chicago Press, 1998), 51–52.

33. Ellery, *Brissot de Warville*, 369–72; see also "Projet de défense devant le tribunal révolutionnaire en réponse au rapport d'Amar," in *J.-P. Brissot, Mémoires*, II: 272–356.

34. Ellery, *Brissot de Warville*, 377–78. Hostile witnesses included Pache, Chaumette, Destournelles, Hébert, Chabot, Montant, Fabre d'Eglantine, Bourdon, Desfaix, and Duhem.

35. Sydenham, *The Girondins*, 28. For a list of those 21 Girondins appearing before the Revolutionary Tribunal on 24 October, see List VII, 218.

36. Ellery, *Brissot de Warville*, 381–82.

37. Sydenham, *The Girondins*, 27–30.

38. Ellery, *Brissot de Warville*, 383–84.

39. Ellery, *Brissot de Warville*, 384–85; see "Anecdotes sur Valazé, Lacaze et Brissot" in M. Guadet, ed., *Mémoires de Buzot* (Paris: Pichon et Didier, Éditeurs, 1828), 192.

40. Ellery, *Brissot de Warville*, 385; Cl. Perroud, ed., *J.-P. Brissot, Correspondance et Papiers* (Paris: Librairie Alphonse Picard & Fils, 1911), 394.

41. Ellery, *Brissot de Warville*, 385–86; Olivier Blanc, *Last Letters: Prisons and Prisoners of the French Revolution, 1793–1794*, trans. Alan Sheridan (New York: Michael di Capua Books, Farrar, Straus and Giroux, 1987), 65.

42. Brissot de Warville, *New Travels*, 6–7.

43. Connelly, *French Revolution*, 138, 142–43.

SIX

Flight of the Fugitives

Of the original group of Girondin fugitives who had gathered in Caen in June 1793, only seven—Buzot, Pétion, Barbaroux, Louvet, Guadet, Salle, and Valady—had managed to reach St. Emilion, where Guadet had relatives. Lesage, Giroux, and Kervélégan had remained behind in Brittany; Larivière was hiding in Falaise; and Gorsas had returned to Paris, where he was arrested and executed. Riouffe, Duchâstel, Girey-Dupré, and Marchena had left for the Bordeaux area ahead of their friends, and they were captured there. Duchâstel and Girey-Dupré were executed, while Riouffe and Marchena were imprisoned in Paris.[1]

For the seven Girondins who had found refuge in St. Emilion, the news of their friends' executions in Paris was devastating. If they had not already felt doomed, they now certainly realized that they could expect neither justice nor mercy from a government that had judged their compatriots so harshly. They reasoned that their only hope was to seek justice posthumously through their memoirs, which they had been writing on the run, from Caen to Quimper, and now in St. Emilion, where they passed the daylight hours underground in an abandoned stone quarry. This same quarry was one among many that once had provided the building materials for Bordeaux and St. Emilion. The quarry could be accessed only by descending into a deep well located in the garden belonging to Thérèse Bouquey, the courageous sister-in-law of Guadet, who was hiding in his father's house nearby. After climbing into the well, it was possible to descend by means of footholds on opposite sides for twenty feet, at which level the well opened into a large cavern; a deeper cave, which could be entered through a hole, was located directly beneath it. Mme. Bouquey furnished the fugitives with a table and chairs, a lantern, and blankets, enabling them to be relatively comfortable underground as they passed the hours writing, talking, and reading. At night they would gather for an evening meal inside the house of their protector, who made the most from her meager allotment of rations. They were in constant danger of discovery from Jacobin agents in the area, but the few months of shelter provided by Mme. Bouquey allowed them enough uninterrupted time to write their personal accounts of recent events.[2]

As arrests and executions escalated in Paris under the government of the Terror, the fugitives realized that their situation had become ever more precarious. They were wanted for treason; thus anyone caught helping them would likewise be accused. Ironically, Buzot earlier had favored a tribunal to judge crimes committed against the nation, and he had spoken about its necessity at a meeting of the Constituent Assembly in 1789. Like his associates, Buzot never had imagined that one day he might be judged a traitor. A respected lawyer, he had even served as the president of such a criminal tribunal in his hometown of Evreux until September 1792, at which time he had been elected as a deputy to the National Convention.[3]

Before the revolution had entered its radical phase, Buzot spoke eloquently regarding the judicial reforms brought about by the revolution. "Individual liberty, without which political liberty is often useless," he declared, "depends upon the institution of the jury." He had also praised the power of public opinion, calling it "the incorruptible safeguard of our liberty." Not long after he began serving in the National Convention, however, Buzot observed that the assembly had become like "an arena of gladiators" as the factions battled each other.[4] Later, during the chaotic spring of 1793, he spoke against the "despotism of the National Convention" and attacked the Paris sections as "anarchists." He had even thought of resigning and returning to Evreux, but he did not want to abandon his friends or to dishonor the oath he had taken to serve his department, so he had remained.[5]

In Saint-Just's report of 8 July, Buzot had been designated as the principal adversary of the Jacobins as well as the instigator of federalism. Then, on 28 July, following the assassination of Marat, the Girondins had been pronounced *hors la loi* or "outside the law." Meanwhile, in Buzot's hometown of Evreux, the order was given to destroy his home and to raise a column condemning him in its place. The contents of his house were removed and sold later at auction.[6]

While it is doubtful that Buzot actually considered establishing federalism in France, evidence does exist indicating that he regarded federalism as a legitimate form of government. The Girondins had, after all, proposed a national referendum on the sentencing of the king, and their distrust of the central government in Paris was widely known. Buzot wrote in his memoir that if the French had realized the true state of the city of Paris before the elections, the Convention would have met elsewhere. He famously described Paris as the "inexhaustible source of all the misfortunes of France" and the cause of "the ruin of this great and sublime revolution." In addition, for the enemies of the Girondins, the 1793 rebellions in Caen, Marseille, Lyon, and Bordeaux served to equate charges of federalism with treason and counter-revolution.[7]

Between August and October 1793, the presence of government authorities and armed troops, sent by the Committee of Public Safety to pacify rebellious areas by all possible means, had increased in the Bordeaux area. The first representatives, Claude-Alexandre Ysabeau and Marc-Antoine Baudot, were sent to Bordeaux in August. Guillaume Chandron-Rousseau and Jean-Lambert Tallien followed in October, along with nearly two thousand armed troops. They threatened to execute anyone "who would make of Bordeaux a new Lyon," a clear reference to Lyon's resistance to the central government and the resulting violence and destruction that followed. The siege of Lyon, begun on 8 August, had led to nine weeks of resistance and the severe punishment of its citizens, nineteen hundred of whom were executed. Caen, on the other hand, had surrendered peacefully to government forces on 3 August. The federalist revolts in Marseille and Bordeaux also had been repressed, although less harshly than in Lyon. Bordeaux, however, would remain under military rule until May 1794; 227 persons were charged with "the crime of federalism" and 104 citizens were executed between October 1793 and May 1794.[8]

By November 1793 Mme. Bouquey had good reason to fear that her protection of the fugitives might be discovered. In addition, her husband in Paris and other relatives had urged her to send them away as soon as possible. On 13 November, therefore, she regretfully told the fugitives that they must seek shelter elsewhere. They had been expecting such an announcement, and after expressing their profound gratitude for her help, the fugitives left their memoirs and other papers in her care; they asked only that she hide the manuscripts until they could be sent safely to the designated persons.

After leaving Mme. Bouquey's house, the friends decided to split up. Buzot, Pétion, and Barbaroux remained together, even returning to Mme. Bouquey's briefly before finding another refuge. Louvet, Guadet, and Salle accompanied Valady for several miles on the road to Périgueux, northeast of Bordeaux, where he hoped to hide in a relative's home. They later learned that Valady had been recognized by the authorities in Périgueux and subsequently executed. For his part, Louvet was determined to travel to Paris, where his wife was hiding with friends. Regardless of the obvious danger, not to say foolhardiness, of such a journey, Louvet took leave of his friends and began walking toward the capital city.[9]

An unlikely hero, Louvet had been aptly described by Manon Roland as "an unhealthy-looking little man, weakly, short-sighted and slovenly." She had added, however, that he was also "as courageous as a lion, simple as a child, a good citizen, and a vigorous writer."[10] He had not received a formal education like the other fugitives, but he had been a voracious reader all his life, had worked in a bookshop, and pursued his goal of becoming a man of letters. First gaining public attention in 1787 with a risqué novel, *Les Amours du Chevalier Faublas*, Louvet continued his literary career throughout the revolution. [11]

In the autumn of 1792, after the assembly had made funds available, Louvet agreed to engage in some propaganda efforts for Interior Minister Roland. He served as the editor of an ardently republican placard-journal, *La Sentinelle*, published twice weekly and distributed throughout Paris. As he had done in his earlier writing, Louvet employed wit and ridicule to confront those who opposed the reforms of the revolution. Later he also worked as the editor of the *Journal des Débats et les Décrets*. [12] Following his election to the National Convention, Louvet had not been shy about criticizing the opponents of the Girondin faction, and he had not hesitated to urge more decisive and unified action on the part of his friends. He had agreed with Manon Roland that the Girondin deputies were moving too slowly against the radical faction in the Convention. [13]

Yet despite his active participation in the government, Louvet remained focused on his personal life and the woman he called Lodoiska. Almost the same age, Louvet and Lodoiska had been childhood friends before they had fallen in love. At the age of sixteen Lodoiska had been forced to marry Mr. Cholet, an older man, but she and Louvet continued to hope that someday they could be united. Louvet had advocated for the right to divorce as well as for priests to marry in a work titled *Emilie de Varmont ou le Divorce Nécssaire*. After 1792, when French civil law legalized divorce, Lodoiska finally had become free to marry Louvet. They were married during the summer of 1793, when the fugitives were on the run in Brittany. Their good friends—Buzot, Pétion, Salle, and Guadet— served as witnesses to the marriage. [14]

When the fugitives left Brittany for St. Emilion, Lodoiska returned to Paris, where she waited to be reunited with Louvet. After leaving Mme. Bouquey's, he had decided to risk going to Paris despite the pleas of his friends to reconsider; he judged that his odds were better on the road to Paris than they would be if he remained in the St. Emilion area. Thus, armed with a false passport, two pistols, and "several pills of excellent opium" hidden in a glove, Louvet set off walking—from St. Emilion to Limoges, Chateauroux, Bourges, Orléans, and finally Paris. His passport identified him as Mr. Larcher, a *sans-culotte* from Rennes, but it lacked the official seals from the various districts on his route. Therefore, he bypassed the larger towns as much as possible and stopped to rest at night in outlying villages. [15]

That Louvet managed to pass as a Jacobin can be attributed to his acting skills as well as to his efforts to placate the local inhabitants. At dinner he never failed to offer his tablemates rounds of wine to ease the conversation. In addition, since he suffered from "rheumatism" in one of his legs, he was fortunate to find drivers who offered to take him as far as they were going. He told one group of passengers that he was a "deserter," and even convinced them to hide him beneath their coats and baggage whenever the wagon stopped at a checkpoint.[16]

Louvet did fear that he might be recognized somewhere along the way, especially as he neared Paris. In Orléans, the capital of the department he had represented in the Convention, he was saddened to see a guillotine erected in the public square and shocked to learn that the executed were known as *Louvetins*. Forced to hide beneath straw and coats for four hours in Orléans while the driver delivered packages, Louvet had been terrified that the guard inspecting the wagon would discover him. Then the next day in Étampes, he underwent the same frightening experience, and again, his luck held. Nevertheless, Louvet's nerves were strained and he was plagued with headaches and fatigue by the time he finally arrived in Paris on 6 December 1793.[17]

Although Louvet realized that he ran an even greater risk of discovery in Paris, he also believed that he could depend on the help of several old friends. One such friend was Citizen Brémont, who had allowed Lodoiska to share his family's home. By the time that Louvet reached Brémont's home that first afternoon, his excitement and relief at reuniting with his wife blinded him to the actual situation. Mme. Brémont had greeted him warmly enough, but she had left the house soon thereafter, and her husband was nowhere in sight. Later that night Louvet was awakened by Lodoiska, who informed him that Brémont wanted him to leave within the hour. Disappointed that an old family friend would treat him so inhospitably, Louvet promised to leave the next day after explaining that it was simply too dangerous to be on the street at night, since he would be stopped and asked to show his identity card. That being the case, Brémont, who did not want to risk being associated with a fugitive, chose to leave his own house.[18]

The next morning Lodoiska left early to look for an apartment to rent in a remote part of the city, while Louvet departed to stay with another old friend, who was more welcoming than Brémont. Lodoiska not only managed to find an apartment but also devised a practical hiding place for her husband inside of one of the walls. Happy to be together despite the constant danger of discovery, the couple lived in their small apartment for two months. When Lodoiska went out to buy food, Louvet retreated into the secret chamber, where he read and wrote by candlelight. At night they barred the door and slept with pistols beneath their pillows.[19]

Meanwhile, as the Terror escalated, Louvet contacted another friend (unnamed in his memoir), one for whom he had done a favor some years before. Now Louvet asked his help in leaving Paris and crossing into Switzerland. The friend, who traveled regularly on business between the two locations, agreed to accompany Louvet. By 6 February 1794 a forged passport and an adequate disguise had been provided, and the two friends were ready to leave. Lodoiska planned to follow in six weeks. Louvet and his friend, both dressed in military attire, walked to Ville-neuve-Saint-Georges, where their papers were examined and they passed without further questions. Louvet also sported "a Jacobin wig of straight black hair . . . and a ferocious moustache," along with a red liberty cap and a large saber. As he had earlier, Louvet was willing to take his chances on reaching Switzerland rather than remaining in Paris and wait-ing to be discovered. He had read the reports about various old friends and associates who had been arrested in Paris and later executed, and he did not wish to be among them.[20]

Louvet and his friend joined a stagecoach en route to Dol, where they arrived the next day and showed their papers to a member of the local committee of surveillance. Louvet reported that he was almost sure that he had been recognized, but for some unknown reason he had been allowed to proceed. They continued walking until they reached the Jura Mountains about five o'clock in the morning. At that point, they parted; Louvet continued walking into Switzerland while his friend hastened back to Paris to reassure Lodoiska. Isolated and lonely but safe in the Swiss mountains, Louvet began to rewrite the memoir that he had begun in St. Emilion.[21] An earlier version of his memoir had covered the period from 1789 to May 1793, when he had been expelled from the Convention.

After six weeks had passed and Lodoiska still had not arrived, Louvet began to imagine that she had been arrested or worse, and according to his memoir, he had even fantasized about turning himself in to save her. Fortunately for his health, which had never been robust, Lodoiska finally appeared in a carriage on 21 May and the couple was able to enjoy a few peaceful months while they waited for the birth of their child. They would return to France only after they had heard the news of Robes-pierre's downfall in late July.[22]

Louvet had been wise as well as lucky. In each hazardous situation in which he had found himself, he had taken the initiative, choosing to leave before it became absolutely necessary. As a consequence of his actions, he became the sole surviving member of the closely knit group that had sought refuge in St. Emilion the previous autumn. Louvet recounted in his memoir that Guadet and Salle had entertained vague plans of escap-ing to Holland or America, but they had not acted on them. Instead, after Louvet left for Paris, they had sought refuge in the St. Emilion home of Guadet's father. They constructed a hiding place inside of a closet, where they could remain secure, even when the elder Guadet received visitors. Thus, rather than attempting to escape from the area, they waited, in essence, for their eventual discovery by the encroaching authorities.[23]

As for Buzot, Pétion, and Barbaroux, due to a combination of poor judgment and misinformation, they also had chosen to remain in the St. Emilion area. They might have escaped from France earlier, when they had been in the Quimper area of Brittany; from there they could have sailed to England instead of choosing to sail down the coast to Bordeaux. They had missed that opportunity, but other options still remained. Their protector, Mme. Bouquey, had been in the process of obtaining forged passports for the fugitives, so that they could travel to Switzerland as Louvet had done. Recent news from Paris, however, had caused them to reconsider leaving the country. When they heard reports that Robespierre and Tallien were engaged in a power struggle in the National Convention, the fugitives reasoned that, if Robespierre's dictatorial rule ended, they might be given the chance to prove their innocence. That such reasoning indicated an unrealistic appraisal of the situation seems obvious in retrospect, but the fugitives persisted in hoping for their eventual pardon. As their memoirs make clear, they were inspired by what they considered the best interests of the nation, and they even envisioned serving again in the national assembly.[24] As subsequent events would show, their decision to remain in St. Emilion was a fatal error.

After Buzot, Pétion, and Barbaroux had left Mme. Bouquey's house in mid-November, they had walked with a guide toward the coast as far as Castillon. Due to a family emergency, however, the guide was unable to accompany them any farther, and they feared to proceed alone, since they did not know a safe route. At that point they decided to retrace their steps and return to Mme. Bouquey's house; a stranger greeted them, warning that it was not safe to remain. On 18 November the authorities had searched the house and the surrounding area, and such *visites domiciliaires* were under way throughout St. Emilion. Retreating to the abandoned stone quarries nearby, the fugitives managed to survive with Mme. Bouquey's help until 21 January 1794, when she found them another hiding place. Their new quarters were in the garret of a house in St. Emilion owned by Baptiste Troquart, a trustworthy wigmaker. Throughout the spring of 1794, Mme. Bouquey continued to supply the three fugitives with food, books, and the news of the day.[25] Remarkably, under the circumstances, Buzot, Pétion, and Barbaroux also were able to meet occasionally with their friends Guadet and Salle and enjoy rare moments of conviviality at the dinner table of Guadet's father.

Their relatively peaceful spring came to an abrupt end in the middle of June. Two local inhabitants, "Coste jeune, a notary, and Nadal, an innkeeper," had reported the presence of the fugitives to a government agent in the area, Marc-Antoine Jullien, who alerted several nearby regiments of cavalry and infantry. On the night of 17 June he directed them to search and occupy all of the houses belonging to the relatives and friends of the Guadet family. The town also was sealed off and no one was allowed to leave. The six men who had searched the home of Guadet's father had found nothing until one of them noticed an irregularity between the ground floor and the attic. Several men climbed up onto the roof, where they discovered the compartment within the closet where Guadet and Salle were hiding. Hearing the men approach, Guadet attempted to shoot himself in the head, but his gun jammed. Both he and Salle, as well as Guadet's father, brother, aunt, and father-in-law, were seized and arrested. The courageous Mme. Bouquey, Guadet's sister-in-law, and her husband likewise were arrested at this time.[26]

By two o'clock the next afternoon, all of those who had been arrested were transported first to Liborne and then to Bordeaux, where they were imprisoned. Indicted before the military commission, not surprisingly they were found guilty. Guadet and Salle were executed on 20 June 1794, to be followed several days later by Guadet's relatives. Reportedly Mme. Bouquey had resisted until her last breath, crying out indignantly, "Bloodthirsty monsters! If humanity, if blood ties are crimes, we all deserve death!"[27]

Buzot, Pétion, and Barbaroux had watched from the garret window as their friends had been taken away from St. Emilion. They reproached themselves for having brought such misfortune upon their benefactor and her family, and feared that Troquart would be treated similarly if they did not leave his house. At midnight on 17 June they slipped out of their hiding place, accompanied briefly by Troquart, who supplied them with bread, meat, and wine before embracing them in farewell. By daybreak they had reached the "plain of Castillon," and there they decided to rest, hidden within a thick pine forest.

The fugitives were not alone, however; a small boy was sitting in a tree nearby, observing the three men as they ate and talked. He watched intently as Barbaroux rose to embrace his companions, then removed a pistol from his pocket and shot himself in the head. The child, surprised and horrified, fell from the tree, picked himself up, and ran away as fast as he could. Believing that Barbaroux had killed himself, Buzot and Pétion also ran from the area and hid in a wheat field some distance away. The child's parents, having been alerted to the scene in the forest, reported it immediately to a police court magistrate in Castillon. The magistrate, accompanied by a surgeon, hurried to the spot where Barbaroux had fallen. Barely alive, the unfortunate fugitive was identified by the papers on his body and carried to Castillon. Despite being near death and unable to speak, Barbaroux was transported by boat to Bordeaux, where Jullien interrogated him. In what must have been a macabre scene, the military commission pronounced "the traitor Barbaroux" guilty and sentenced him to be guillotined; on 25 June 1794, the twenty-seven-year-old former Girondin deputy from Marseille was duly executed.[28]

Despairing of escape or refuge, Buzot and Pétion apparently decided to end their own lives as well. Although no one actually witnessed their deaths, the two bodies were found in a wheat field, their faces half-eaten by wolves but still recognizable. They were buried where they had fallen in the area known as the Field of the Émigrés.[29]

As noted earlier, the fugitives had given their memoirs and other "diverse papers" to Mme. Bouquey for safekeeping, and she, in turn, had placed the materials in a tin box. Fearing that she could be arrested at any time, she had then deposited the tin box in the latrine, where she assumed that it would not be noticed. A domestic servant had observed her actions, however, and dutifully passed on the information to the authorities; they were reportedly "delighted" with the discovery. Fortunately for historians, the contents of the tin box were turned over to Jullien and later deposited in the national library and archives.[30]

In addition to the fugitives' memoirs, which provided individual perspectives on revolutionary events, the tin box also contained a "declaration of principles" written by Buzot and Pétion. Intended for their fellow citizens as well as for later generations, the declaration serves as a final statement of their idealistic hopes for the revolution and their consequent disappointment at its degeneration. They began by condemning the system of hereditary monarchy, "a principal source of errors . . . that has degraded men for centuries," and hailed a system that respected the rights of man as originally set forth in the Constituent Assembly: "We have defended, as much as it has been in our power, these eternal principles based on reason, morality and justice. It is on these foundations that we wished to establish a wise and durable liberty." The turning point of the revolution had been the September massacres, they wrote, those "days of crime," when men with the basest morals were elevated to the most important posts. These men, according to Buzot and Pétion, formed a faction that gained strength "by the most odious means," and who finally became dominant through "the audacity of their heinous crimes." Their ascendancy chased away "the talented and good men," an obvious reference to themselves as Girondin leaders.

Emphasizing their "constant efforts" to halt the progress of "this liberticide faction," the writers also blamed themselves, "the weakness of a party of our own colleagues and the silence and stupor of the nation," for making the situation worse. The Girondins, they explained, had not chosen to seek a "false popularity," but instead had opted to follow their consciences, despite the ingratitude of the people they served. While they had been disappointed that the people in the provinces had lacked the will to rise up against the government in Paris, they also acknowledged that the Girondins had remained too divided to act forcefully against their enemies.

Finally, Buzot and Pétion admitted that when they had been hiding in Brittany, they could easily have escaped to England, but they had chosen to remain in their own country to the end. "We think, therefore, that our political life in the revolution is exempt from all reproaches," they declared, and challenged their enemies to prove otherwise. They closed this last testament by despairing that "liberty is lost. We can no longer render any service to our country. . . . We have resolved to give up our lives and to no longer be witnesses to the slavery that is going to desolate our unfortunate country." They ended by commending their memoirs to "good people and friends of truth and liberty."[31] Since this declaration had been written earlier in November, while they were still hiding at Mme. Bouquey's, apparently they had determined even then to take their own lives rather than risk capture by the enemy.

It is worth recalling that earlier in the revolution, during the period of the Constituent Assembly, the Rolands' circle of friends meeting weekly in their apartment had included not only Buzot and Pétion but Robespierre as well. At that time Madame Roland had famously referred to the three deputies as "the incorruptibles," a label that had come to refer finally, and ironically, only to Robespierre.[32]

Now, in the terrible final months of the revolution, Robespierre still remained, although his popularity among the government leaders had decreased, and "the incorruptible" was more feared than admired. He could not have been unaware of the forces gathering against him, especially after Vadier and Amar had charged him with associating with a mystical cult suspected of having Catholic and royalist ties. Catherine Théot, the leader known as the "Mother of God," had publicly referred to Robespierre as the "True Messiah," a title that under less precarious circumstances might have appealed to the moralistic leader. The charge was later dropped, but members of the Committee of Public Safety had not agreed on the decision. Consequently, Fouché, Chaumette, Barras, Fréron, Tallien, and others began organizing the National Convention against Robespierre.[33]

Some in the Convention feared, with good reason, that Robespierre might turn against them just as he had earlier turned against Danton, who had then been executed. Nevertheless, although they had passed the Law of 22 Prairial both despite and because of their fears, the deputies realized that some action must be taken soon to thwart Robespierre's dictatorial powers. Beginning in mid-June, however, Robespierre withdrew from public view, remaining in his rooms for the next six weeks. His absence, whether from ill health or quarrels with other deputies, led to the neglect of his work for the Committee of Public Safety, thus weakening his position and playing into his enemies' hands.[34]

On 26 July (8 Thermidor on the revolutionary calendar) Robespierre finally chose to emerge and address the Convention. Consisting of thirty closely printed pages and taking two hours to deliver, Robespierre's diatribe accused others of calumny and conspiracy while praising his own virtue and efforts to save the country.[35] As he was speaking, he also held a list of unread names in one hand, causing his audience to assume that it was an "enemies list." They reasoned that they could not afford to wait until he made the list public, and began planning their next course of action.

The next day, known as 9 Thermidor, Robespierre and Saint-Just appeared before the Convention again, but this time they were interrupted repeatedly. Cries of "Down with the tyrant!" and "Out with the Dictator!" rang out. At the same time Tallien warned that an army under Hanriot, commander of the Paris National Guard, was forming to support Robespierre. Chaos reigned in the assembly hall as Robespierre attempted to speak in his own defense. Few cared to listen any longer to the words of "the Incorruptible." By the time the tumult subsided, the deputies had voted to arrest not only Robespierre but also his brother Augustin, Saint-Just, and Couthon, all members of the Committee of Public Safety, as well as Hanriot and Dumas, head of the Revolutionary Tribunal, and others, all of whom were hurried away to various prisons. By ten o'clock that night, however, the four most important prisoners (Robespierre, Augustin, Saint-Just, and Couthon) had been released and transported, with the Commune's help, to the Hotel de Ville (city hall), where they waited while the Convention sat in emergency session.[36]

The Paris Commune still wielded sufficient military strength to attack the Convention, but its members lacked enough political will to do so effectively; only a quarter of the sections (16 of 48) responded to the call for action. Without the necessary support of the populace, Robespierre and his associates could do nothing to defend themselves. The Convention, meanwhile, had declared Robespierre an outlaw, which meant that if he tried to escape, he could be shot by anyone. The deputies also "reordered" the arrest of those previously arrested as well as the "entire insurrectionary Commune." At 2:30 that morning, Convention guards joined National Guardsmen from local sections at the Hotel de Ville, where they forced their way into the upper room holding the outlaws. In a panic, Robespierre tried to kill himself, but the bullet only hit his jaw, causing severe pain and bleeding. His brother Augustin jumped from the window, while the wheelchair-bound Couthon fell down the stairs. Saint-Just had remained seated, perhaps in a state of shock at the situation confronting him. All four men were captured, regardless of their physical condition, and restrained, while the Committees of Public Safety and Public Security engaged in a half-hearted hearing in the Tuileries. The prisoners were not tried. Instead, the following afternoon, Robespierre, Saint-Just, and Couthon were executed, followed by Augustin and eighteen of their followers. On 29 July seventy-one more "Robespierristes," most from the Commune, were guillotined.[37]

The executions of Robespierre and his followers effectively ended the period of the Terror and altered the course of the revolution. The "Thermidorian Reaction" of 1794–1795 would see the establishment of a less authoritarian government with the National Convention back in charge. The deputies moved quickly, repealing the Law of Prairial on 1 August and releasing suspects who had been seized under that law on 5 August, including five hundred prisoners in Paris alone. On 10 August, the Revolutionary Tribunal was reorganized as a special court for treason cases and some moderate judges were added. The new Tribunal would acquit 132 prisoners during the autumn of 1794.[38]

NOTES

1. John Rivers, *Louvet: Revolutionist and Romance-Writer* (London: Hurst and Blackett, Ltd., 1910), 223–26; Owen Connelly, *French Revolution/Napoleonic Era* (New York: Holt, Rinehart and Winston, 1979), 138–40.

2. Rivers, *Louvet*, 269–71, 330. For a detailed account of the fugitives in St. Emilion, see Bette W. Oliver, *Orphans on the Earth: Girondin Fugitives from the Terror, 1793–1794* (Lanham, Md.: Lexington Books, 2009).

3. Jacques Hérissay, *Un Girondin, François Buzot, Député de l'Eure à l'Assemblée Constituante et à la Convention, 1760–1794* (Paris: Librairie Académique, Perrin et Cie., Libraires-Éditeurs, 1907), 62, 152.

4. Hérissay, *Un Girondin, François Buzot*, 161, 237.

5. Hérissay, *Un Girondin, François Buzot*, 288, 282, 290; François-Nicolas-Louis Buzot, *Mémoires de F.-N.-L. Buzot, Membre de l'Assemblée Constituante et député à la Convention Nationale par le département de l'Eure, Année 1793*, N. A. F. 1730, 32 (Paris: Bibliothèque Nationale, Dept. des Manuscrits).

6. Hérissay, *Un Girondin, François Buzot*, 332–33. The inscription on the column read, "Ici fut l'asile du scélèrat Buzot, qui, représentant du peuple, conspira la perte de la République française."

7. M. J. Sydenham, *The Girondins* (London: University of London, Athlone Press, 1961), 194–96; Buzot, *Mémoires*, N.A. F. 1730, 78, 71–72.

8. W. D. Edmonds, *Jacobinism and the Revolt of Lyon, 1789–1793* (New York: Oxford University Press, 1990), 267–71, 280; Rivers, *Louvet*, 257; Paul R. Hanson, *The Jacobin Republic under Fire: The Federalist Revolt in the French Revolution* (University Park: Pennsylvania State University Press, 2003), 226–27, 230–31, 193.

9. Rivers, *Louvet*, 273–78; C. A. Dauban, ed., *Mémoires Inédits de Pétion et Mémoires de Buzot & de Barbaroux, accompagnés de Notes Inédites de Buzot et de nombreux documents inédits sur Barbaroux, Buzot, Brissot, etc.* (Paris: Henri Plon, 1866), 493.

10. Rivers, *Louvet*, 269–71, 330.

11. Leigh Whaley, *Radicals: Politics and Republicanism in the French Revolution* (London: Sutton Publishing Ltd., 2000), 9.

12. Rivers, *Louvet*, 17.

13. Jean-Baptiste Louvet, *Mémoires de J.-B. Louvet, l'un des Représentans Proscrits en 1793*, N. A. F. 1730, 154, 156 (Paris: Bibliothèque Nationale, Dept. des Manuscrits).

14. Rivers, *Louvet*, 221–22; Louvet, *Mémoires*, N.A. F. 1730, 144.

15. Jean-Baptiste Louvet, *Mémoires de J.-B. Louvet, auteur de Faublas, membre de la Convention, etc., de la Journée du 31 Mai, suivis de Quelques Notices pour l'Histoire et le Récit de Mes Périls depuis cette Epoque Jusqu'à la Rentrée des Députés Proscrits dans l'Assemblée Nationale* (Paris: a la Librairie Historique, 1821), 78–84, 92–93.

16. Louvet, *Mémoires de J.-B. Louvet, auteur de Faublas*, 108, 119–25.

17. Louvet, *Mémoires de J.-B. Louvet, auteur de Faublas*, 138–58. The Girondins were also variously referred to as Brissotins, Buzotins, Rolandins, and so forth.

18. Louvet, *Mémoires de J.-B. Louvet, auteur de Faublas*, 160–68.

19. Louvet, *Mémoires de J.-B. Louvet, auteur de Faublas*, 172–90.

20. Louvet, *Mémoires de J.-B. Louvet, auteur de Faublas*, 184–207. In his memoir Louvet mentioned the discoveries of Clavière, Rabaut, Bois-Guyon, Girey-Dupré, Custine, Mazuyer, and Valady.

21. Louvet, *Mémoires de J.-B. Louvet, auteur de Faublas*, 208–15.

22. Louvet, *Mémoires de J.-B. Louvet, auteur de Faublas*, 215–30.

23. Dauban, ed., *Mémoires Inédits de Pétion*, 494–97.

24. Dauban, ed., *Mémoires Inédits de Pétion*, 498–99; Connelly, *French Revolution*, 163. For a detailed discussion of the fugitives' memoirs, see Oliver, *Orphans on the Earth*.

25. Dauban, ed., *Mémoires Inédits de Pétion*, 498.

26. Dauban, ed., *Mémoires Inédits de Pétion*, 499–500.

27. Dauban, ed., *Mémoires Inédits de Pétion*, 502, 508n1.

28. Dauban, ed., *Mémoires Inédits de Pétion*, 502–3, 508.

29. Dauban, ed. *Mémoires Inédits de Pétion*, 503; Rivers, *Louvet*, 282.

30. Dauban, ed., *Mémoires Inédits de Pétion*, xliv, 505.

31. Dauban, ed., *Mémoires Inédits de Pétion*, 505, xliv–xlviii.

32. Gita May, *Madame Roland and the Age of Revolution* (New York: Columbia University Press, 1970), 182–83.

33. Connelly, *French Revolution*, 163–64.

34. John Hardman, *Robespierre* (London: Longman, 1999), 174–75, 181.

35. Richard T. Bienvenu, *The Ninth of Thermidor: The Fall of Robespierre* (Oxford: Oxford University Press, 1968), 143–74; J. M. Roberts and John Hardman, eds., *French Revolution Documents* (Oxford: Blackwell, 1973), 256–57.

36. Connelly, *French Revolution*, 164–65; David Andress, *The Terror: The Merciless War for Freedom in Revolutionary France* (New York: Farrar, Straus and Giroux, 2005), 332–41.

37. Connelly, *French Revolution*, 165–66; Andress, *The Terror*, 341–45.

38. Connelly, *French Revolution*, 168–69.

SEVEN

Those Who Survived

Among those released from prison was the journalist Honoré Riouffe, who had first been arrested on 4 October 1793 along with Duchâstel and Marchena, the Spaniard who had tried to help Brissot earlier that June. Riouffe, Duchâstel, and Marchena had accompanied the Girondin fugitives to Brittany and then had gone on ahead of the others to Bordeaux, where they were subsequently captured. Duchâstel was later executed, while Riouffe and Marchena were imprisoned in Paris on 16 October 1793. In his riveting memoir Riouffe presented an eyewitness account of prison life in Paris from October 1793 to July 1794. As a journalist, he chose to include details about both the prisoners and their guards that serve to enlarge the perspective of that period and add to a better understanding of it.[1] Riouffe made no pretense of objectivity, however, instead choosing to present an emotionally charged and obviously biased account of what he had seen.

Explaining that he had never before appeared before a magistrate, Riouffe did not know what to expect. Thrown into a dungeon along with a crowd of "unfortunates," he realized for the first time what others before him had suffered. After interrogation, Riouffe and Marchena, on their way to the carriages that would transport them separately to Paris, passed by their friend Duchâstel, his hands and feet in irons. Escorted by Jacobin guards, "complete with fierce moustaches, sabers, pistols, and red liberty caps," Riouffe remarked that "liberty had not given them any idea of the dignity of man." Upon their arrival in Paris, the two prisoners were paraded for three hours at all the prisons in the city, from the Luxembourg to La Force and l'Abbaye before they were finally taken to the Conciergerie. Fatigued and cramped after 149 hours in the carriages, the prisoners were separated and placed in cells with "robbers, counterfeiters, and assassins." Riouffe reported that three guards with enormous dogs visited his cell at night. Suspected of being a Brissotin, he kept silent for the first thirteen days and tried to lose himself in dreams and in composing poetry. Falling into a depressed state, he wrote that he ate little, because food only served to agitate his spirit.[2]

At eleven o'clock one morning, Riouffe was taken from his cell for an interrogation. He described himself, after thirteen days in prison, as "a deplorable spectacle: pale, defeated, with a long, dirty beard, and clothing covered with pieces of straw from my bed." He was then moved to another part of the prison, which he called "the temple of persecuted virtue," where his former Girondin associates were housed. There he met again Vergniaud, Gensonné, Brissot, Ducos, Fonfrède, Valazé, Duchâstel, and others. Riouffe discovered that Ducos had urged his transfer from the "den of criminals," and he was grateful to be surrounded once more by men whom he greatly admired. Unfortunately, within two days these Girondins would be condemned to die, and Riouffe would find himself facing increased desolation.[3]

During the brief period that he shared with the Girondins, Riouffe took note of their calm demeanor as they awaited execution. He quoted La Source as saying to his judges after his condemnation, "I am murdered at the moment when the people have lost their reason; you, you will be murdered when they have recovered it."[4] Brissot he described as "grave and reflective," while Gensonné disdained speaking about his assassins and chose to reflect on the condition of the people he had vowed to represent. Vergniaud, "grave and serious," recited some verses, and sometimes the others joined in. Riouffe wrote that he regretted the imminent loss of such "sublime eloquence." As for Valazé, he "smiled serenely" and appeared to be already freed from his earthly bonds; therefore, Riouffe was not surprised to learn that after being condemned, Valazé had stabbed himself with a pair of scissors that he had hidden under his coat. Vergniaud, for his part, took poison rather than face execution. Riouffe also described the youth and deep friendship of "the two brothers, Fonfrède and Ducos," and their tears at the thoughts of leaving their wives, children, and life itself.[5]

On 30 October, the night that the Girondin prisoners were condemned, Riouffe recalled that they sang patriotic chants until the daylight hours. He despaired that so many extraordinary men—"their youth, beauty, character, virtues, and talent"—should be *massacré en masse*. They were, he wrote, "exalted by their courage" and died well as they had lived. For Riouffe, however, their faces seemed to remain before him, and the places they had occupied became "objects of religious veneration." He was haunted by their spirits and felt obliged to honor "the best of our citizens," comparable to Cato ad Brutus.[6]

The day before their executions Riouffe reported that Madame Roland had arrived at the women's section of the Conciergerie, which was separated from the men's section by an iron grille. She appeared calm and elegant, with "a very spiritual face," but her misfortunes had left "traces of melancholy." According to Riouffe, she spoke often to the other prisoners at the grille with "the liberty and courage of a great man." He found that such republican language coming from the mouth of a pretty French woman waiting to be executed was "one of the miracles of the revolution." Her conversation was serious without being cold, he wrote, and she always spoke of the condemned deputies with respect, calling them "our friends." On the day of her interrogation she appeared assured, but afterward those who saw her noticed that her eyes were wet; as we know, she had not been allowed to defend herself from the "outrageous questions" asked by her interrogators. Riouffe wrote that on the day of her execution, Madame Roland had dressed in white, "a symbol of the purity of her soul." Her death, coming so soon after that of his Girondin friends, only deepened Riouffe's despair.[7]

Turning to the fate of his other associates, Riouffe wrote that Clavière, Brissot's good friend and financial supporter, had stabbed himself, and soon after his wife had taken poison. Girey-Dupré and Boisguyon, who had arrived at the Conciergerie from Bordeaux, had been interrogated, condemned, and executed. Riouffe regretted the loss of Girey-Dupré, who had served as the editor of the *Patriote Français* following Brissot's election to the National Convention, calling his death "an irreparable crime" for the country. In his memoir, Riouffe included a poem written by Girey-Dupré before his execution; it was titled *L'immortalité nous attend*. As for Boisguyon, Riouffe described him as "a practical philosopher . . . but his spirit was not as elevated as that of Girey-Dupré."[8]

Turning to the last days of other revolutionary figures, Riouffe wrote that Bailly, the former mayor of Paris, had been abandoned by the people who had once honored him, even comparing his disgraceful end to that of Plato or Jesus. Camille Desmoulins, a man with "much imagination and poor judgment," according to Riouffe, had been "furious to have been the dupe of Robespierre." He even praised Desmoulins for daring to offer clemency at least once during the Terror. The "terrible" Danton, for his part, seemed to be somewhat ashamed to have been fooled by Robespierre. Riouffe devoted several pages to Danton's words, as he remembered them. Placed in a cell next to Westerman, Danton had asked pardon of God and man for the revolutionary tribunals with which he had intended to prevent more September massacres. He had also speculated that things could have turned out differently: Brissot could have guillotined the Jacobins! Danton acknowledged that he had spies, and knew he would be arrested. He had called Robespierre "a Nero" and declared, "In revolutions, authority rests with the scoundrels; and it is better to be a poor sinner than a governor of men." Riouffe added that Danton spoke constantly about nature, especially the trees in the countryside where he had a home. In his opinion, Danton "had the instinct of the great, but not of genius"; he could imagine, but not direct.[9]

Riouffe wrote that Fabre d'Eglantine, who was sick and weak, seemed to be only concerned about his comedy in five acts that he had left in the hands of the Committee of Public Safety; apparently he feared that Billaud-Varenne might steal it. Cloots died as he had lived, "the personal enemy of Jesus Christ," but with more courage than expected, according to Riouffe, while Hébert, "that scandalous fabrication of filth," appeared weak and humiliated.[10]

Toward the end of his memoir of confinement, Riouffe wondered why he had been witness to so much misery, noting that as a result, he had "terrible memories" of all the unfortunates who had passed before his eyes. Before 22 Prairial, he wrote, the revolutionary tribunals had at least followed some prescribed forms, but then it had turned into "a tribunal of blood" composed of assassins. Some victims had been condemned by mistake, due to the laziness of the half-literate subordinates checking names and evidence; he wrote that the records would offer proof of their errors. As for the jurors, Riouffe declared that most were vile and lowly, wearing "masks of virtue."[11]

The Conciergerie had become even more "hellish" during the last month of his captivity. Day and night they arrived, he reported, sixty at a time, from all over France, to be replaced the next day by one hundred others. "Mandates of death" were distributed to sixty to eighty persons each day, frightening six hundred others in the process. Toward three o'clock in the afternoon, the long processions of victims descended from the Tribunal, walking slowly under the long arches, watched avidly by the other prisoners. Riouffe reported that he had seen "forty-five magistrates from the Parlement of Paris, thirty-three from the Parlement of Toulouse, going to their deaths, as well as thirty farmers-general pass by with calm and firm steps." He had watched generals, "their laurels changed to cypress," and young soldiers "so strong and vigorous," surrounded by guards, seemingly rendered immobile as if struck dumb by the judgments they had received. They walked silently, resigned to their deaths.[12]

Riouffe observed that the victims were mixed together, regardless of their former ranks in society, while sometimes entire generations were destroyed in one day. He cited the highly respected eighty-year-old Malesherbes, who perished with his family, and four members of Brienne's family who died together. He mentioned fourteen young girls from Verdun and twenty women from Poitou, poor peasants for the most part, who waited "like cows crowded together in the market" for their executions. Some women had died in the cart en route to Paris, he reported, but their cadavers were still guillotined.[13]

Noting that his epoch had offered examples of all kinds of crimes but also sometimes "sublime virtue," Riouffe described young *femmes-de-chambre* who chose to die with their mistresses as well as a good monk who refused to save his life by lying; the former marquise de Bois-Bérenger, who refused to leave her mother for an instant; and the former comtesse Malézy, who consoled her father. He wrote that all of these families who died together believed that they were destined for a better world in eternity, but first they were forced to endure the ordeal of preparation for their executions and the reception of the furious populace. After witnessing so many unfortunate victims during his months of captivity, Riouffe wrote that his soul had been poisoned by despair, and he "would die ashamed to have been a man."[14]

At the end of his memoir Riouffe included a revealing letter, dated 5 Ventose, An 3, to Joseph Souque, who had been arrested with Brissot in Moulins and released after 9 Thermidor. He admitted to Souque that he had lived in fear that he might cause the death of a friend who had come to visit him or one that had inquired about him. Such fear, he wrote, consumed him day and night for eleven months, "like a rodent gnawing at his heart." Vowing that he was ready to die at any moment, Riouffe praised the examples of courage shown by his Girondin associates as well as by those early Roman heroes—Cassius, Brutus, and Cato. Despite his inner torment, Riouffe wrote, he had tried to appear calm and counsel others when possible.[15]

The object of his letter, according to Riouffe, was to show his friend the interior of the prison where he had witnessed so much sadness and courage. He informed Souque that he had inhabited cell number thirteen, which contained eighteen beds separated by high planks; he noted that the candles cast ominous shadows on the walls. Riouffe wrote that he had felt fortunate to share a cell with "S—, the brave commander from Finistère who had saved the National Convention on 10 March." He also mentioned "a good Benedictine . . . always with his hands joined on his chest, as in a painting of St. Benoit," who offered his sufferings to God. Some of the other prisoners, however, chose to irritate the good monk by chanting to another god they named Ibrascha. The monk would pretend to be asleep, but when he could tolerate their blasphemies no longer, he would chant *De Profundis* in return. Riouffe reported that, despite their annoying chants, the other prisoners actually respected the monk, and he knew it.[16]

In the midst of their somber surroundings there were occasional moments of some merriment as well as philosophical discussions to occupy the long hours. "This mixture of diverse sentiments," Riouffe decided, "only proved that human existence resembled a delirious dream." The prisoners would sing sometimes and compose chants while they ate, eighteen to twenty to a table, some of whom might be eating their last meal. They improvised Socrates' apology, reciting it with great feeling, he reported, noting that deism seemed to replace superstition as death neared, even for self-proclaimed atheists. Because humanity has need of hope and consolation at such times, the prisoners shared a "touching friendship" as they waited for what each new day would bring.[17]

Riouffe told Souque that after he had been freed and returned to society, nothing surprised him more than the "curtness" and "coldness" that he found. Those in the outside world had no idea, it seemed, of what he and the other prisoners had endured, nor did they seem to care. In ancient times, he wrote, the traveler was welcome to recite his adventures and the audience listened eagerly, but for him, who had traveled "toward the end of life," there seemed to be little interest. He explained that was one of the reasons for writing the letter as well as his prison memoir. Despair, he wrote, envelopes those who are imprisoned and deprived of their liberty, and men in such a state of crisis are without consolation. For fourteen months he had lived under the threat of death, yet he had not died of sorrow. Rather, "I have lived because each instant I believed that I was going to cease living." [18]

Riouffe ended his letter by mentioning that he had enclosed some of his "stanzas," composed before 9 Thermidor to please his "comrades in misfortune." They had recited them often to raise their spirits, he reported, and he hoped that the stanzas would bear witness to the courage of those in cell number thirteen. [19] Riouffe also included a few pages to explain the false religion of Ibrascha, with which the prisoners in cell number 13 had tormented the Benedictine monk. The twenty-five *Maximes d'Ibrascha* mocked not only religion but the extreme measures of the revolution as well, and they must have injected some welcome moments of humor into the lives of most of those involved. [20]

Some *Pieces Diverses* are included at the end of Riouffe's memoir, including Madame Roland's defense and a fragment from an undated letter from the Girondin deputy Guadet's widow to one of her friends. In it, the *Veuve Guadet* described the irreparable loss of "the dearest of husbands" as well as that of her seventy-eight-year-old father, her sister Madame Bouquey, her father-in-law, a brother-in-law, and one of her aunts at the hands of "monsters" and "cannibals." She described being taken to the tribunal, along with her three children, and then being released and feeling abandoned by all. Even her doctor had abandoned her, she wrote. Such was "the fear that filled everyone's heart at the time." [21]

Madame Guadet was only one of the Girondin widows that had suffered loss and abandonment at the hands of the radical government of 1793–1794. Although a law on restitution had been adopted on 29 May 1795, it often proved difficult to determine to whom and how much should be allotted to the families of the victims of the Terror. There were many exceptions, including the obvious ones such a émigrés or members of the royal family.

By the autumn of 1795, general opinion on the Girondins had shifted dramatically in their favor. Those who had survived, including Louvet, were readmitted to the Convention, while those who had died were hailed as "martyrs of liberty." A special celebration in their memory was held on 3 October, during which all of the deputies wore crepe on their arms. A funeral urn in the assembly hall bore the following inscription: "To the magnanimous defenders of liberty, who died in prison or upon the scaffold during the tyranny." The president of the Convention eloquently recalled the martyred representatives of the people and "their constant courage and their tragic end."[22] The Convention dissolved itself on 26 October 1795, and the new legislature composed of seven hundred and fifty deputies took its place. The first Directory, led by Barras, Carnot, Le Tourneur, Reubell, and Révellière-Lépaux, would serve until the elections of 1796–1797.

By April 1796, the government had tried to make some sort of restitution to the widows and children of those martyred Girondins. The official decree declared, "Considering that Valazé, Pétion, Carra, Buzot, Gorsas, Brissot, members of the National Convention, are of those representatives of the people who, having cooperated to establish liberty and to found the Republic, sealed it with their blood, and died victims of their devotion to the country and of their respect for the rights of the nation," each of their widows should have a pension of 2,000 francs a year for herself, and the same amount for each of her children until they reached the age of fifteen.[23]

Those Girondin widows who had endured poverty and disgrace after their husbands had been proscribed in June 1793 welcomed any assistance that the government might be inclined to provide. Madame Buzot, for example, had lost her home in Evreux, which was razed following her husband's flight to Caen in the summer of 1793. Buzot had worried that his death would leave his childless wife destitute; therefore, in July 1793, he had given her the power of attorney to manage his affairs. Despite Buzot's intention that she would be compensated for whatever losses she had suffered because of him, Madame Buzot received only the small pension allotted to the Girondin widows (in her case, approximately 666 livres). She died at Evreux on 30 July 1812. Pétion's wife had fared little better. She received about the same amount as Madame Buzot. Both she and her son had been imprisoned for a short time in Sainte-Pélagie, while her mother, accused of royalism, had been guillotined. Her son became a cavalry officer, and in 1823 he returned to Chartres to dispose of his remaining "mediocre paternal heritage."[24]

Madame Brissot had been forced to leave her Paris apartment after her husband was imprisoned in June 1793. She and their three children had wandered about seeking refuge in various places until she was arrested and imprisoned with her youngest son at La Force from 30 October 1793 to 19 February 1794. Her mother, Madame Dupont, took care of the two older children during that traumatic period. Later, when Madame Brissot was able to reclaim the contents of her Paris apartment, including Brissot's library, she was saddened to find that some things were missing. She estimated that her expenses for the past year plus the value of the missing items amounted to 80,510 francs, and she asked the government to reimburse her. For its part, the government agreed to make a payment of 55,000 francs "for the property which had been taken from her during the imprisonment of her husband," but declined to pay the amount that she had requested.[25]

With the decree of 26 April 1796, Madame Brissot and the children were awarded a pension, but they continued to experience financial difficulties. In 1799, along with her mother and sisters, she attempted to open a school in Versailles, but the project was not successful. She did manage finally to partially improve her situation by running "a reading-room or bookshop" at number seven, rue du Commerce, in Paris. To add to her difficulties, Madame Brissot's children were also a source of some anxiety. She had complained earlier that their father's focus of attention on political matters rather than on his family had resulted in poorly disciplined children. Sylvain, the middle son, had gone to America in 1816, but he did not share his father's or his uncle's enthusiasm for the United States and found the "crude manners" of Americans disgusting. He failed in his efforts to support himself by teaching French and mathematics, fell into a depression, and died penniless in 1819. The oldest son, Felix, had enjoyed a career in the "marine service," but he died in Saint-Domingue. Anacharsis, the youngest and most successful of the Brissot children, served as a military officer under the First Empire and owned property in the department of the Yonne. Exhausted by all that she had endured, Félicité Brissot died in 1818, and thanks to the generosity of her sister Nancy, she was buried at the Père Lachaise cemetery in Paris.[26]

Jean-Baptiste Louvet had been among those surviving Girondins who returned to serve in the Convention. He wanted to ensure that his friends who had perished as fugitives would be remembered and awarded the respect he thought they deserved. He lost no time reminding the other members of the Convention about his friends, even reading the "last letters" of Buzot, Pétion, and Barbaroux, which had been entrusted to their protector Troquart for safekeeping. The "last letters," brief and heartfelt as they were, produced just the desired emotional effect on the deputies that he had anticipated, according to Louvet. He also read aloud a petition by Citizen Troquart, in which the wig-maker described himself as a victim of tyranny, an inhabitant of St. Emilion, where "your unfortunate colleagues, Guadet, Buzot, Pétion, Barbaroux and Salle perished." He explained that he had hidden and fed Buzot, Pétion, and Barbaroux for five months, and as a result he had been imprisoned for eight months. Declaring that he had always been poor, Troquart claimed that he had used up his meager resources by providing for the fugitives. Finally, he left it to the discretion of the deputies "to accord me that which appears just to you." After Louvet had read the "last letters" and the petition from Troquart, he proposed a decree that would include a payment of 1,500 livres to Troquart and the deposit of the letters in the national library.

Subsequently, however, Troquart received only a small portion of the amount suggested by Louvet.[27]

Tireless in his efforts, Louvet had proposed another decree in the Convention on 11 March 1795. The decree declared, "All republicans who had taken up arms in protest of June 2 [the expulsion of the Girondins from the Convention] had served their country well."[28] The proposal was not accepted, but nevertheless Louvet continued to work on behalf of his martyred friends and their families.

When Louvet, his wife Lodoiska, and their infant son returned to Paris after 9 Thermidor, he had discovered that much of his property had been stolen. Soon, however, he managed to establish a combination bookshop and publishing business in an office in the Palais Royal. In addition to his own memoir, *Récit de Mes Périls*, in 1795 he also published Madame Roland's memoir, *Appel à l'impartiale postérité*, in four volumes; it was edited by her longtime friend Bosc. The proceeds from her memoir were reserved for Eudora, the Rolands' orphaned daughter.[29]

Even when he had been younger Louvet had not enjoyed robust health, and after 1795 he grew even weaker. Elected to the Council of Five Hundred, the legislative successor to the National Convention, Louvet represented the department of Haute-Vienne until May 1797. Increasingly disillusioned by the increase of royalist strength within the government, he decided to seek a diplomatic post instead. By the time that he received an appointment as consul in Palermo in August 1797, however, he was too ill to accept it. Louvet died, only thirty-seven years of age, on 25 August. Worn out by the challenges he had dealt with during the revolution combined with his already poor health, he had somehow managed to survive long enough to enjoy at least some satisfaction in his accomplishments. He had also been fortunate to share his life with the clever and practical Lodoiska, who continued to manage her husband's business interests until her death in 1814. Their son, unlike his parents, led a reclusive life in Montargis in the department of the Loiret, where he died in 1846.[30]

In a sense these survivors also had become victims of the revolution. Their lives had been altered dramatically and they had suffered not only physical privations but also the severing of emotional ties. From Riouffe, who apparently experienced at least some survivor's guilt, to the widows and children of the Girondin martyrs, survival did not guarantee that their lives would markedly improve.

Yet not all of the survivors suffered such difficult afterlives. For example, the LeBruns, David, and Marguerite Gérard, although certainly affected by the changes brought about by the revolution, continued successfully to pursue their careers in the arts. Elisabeth Vigée-LeBrun returned to Paris on 18 January 1802, taking up residence in the home she had shared with her former husband on the rue du Gros Chênet. This action reinforces the idea that LeBrun had divorced her in 1792 in order to protect his property. She wrote in her memoir that Paris seemed sad to her, while its narrow streets did not compare favorably with those wide boulevards of St. Petersburg and Berlin. Noting a visit from Josephine, Madame Bonaparte, whom she had known before the revolution, Vigée-LeBrun reported that when she finally saw Bonaparte in person, she was surprised at his small size. She had imagined him, much as she had Catherine II of Russia, to be of a stature appropriate to his accomplishments.[31]

Unable to re-create the pre-revolutionary atmosphere she remembered, Vigée-LeBrun alternated between living in Paris and in a country house near Meudon, where she completed several portraits begun earlier in Russia and Germany. In December, after asking LeBrun to return her dowry, she began using her maiden name in legal contracts, and since they were legally divorced, LeBrun could not refuse.[32] Following the Peace Treaty of Amiens in April 1803, Vigée-LeBrun departed for London, where she rejoiced to see again her old friends, the Comte de Vaudreuil and the Comte d'Artois. While she felt little affinity for the city of London, she remained there until the summer of 1805 and painted portraits of such notables as the Prince of Wales and Lord Byron.[33]

In July 1805, Vigée-LeBrun returned to Paris, where she resumed an active social and professional life, but she left again in 1807, this time to visit Madame de Staël in Switzerland. Before she left, however, she had helped her former husband settle many of his debts. In exchange, she received mortgages on his real properties and bought from him the Hôtel de Lubert, its outbuildings and gardens. Throughout their marriage and even after the divorce, Vigée-LeBrun continued to help her husband financially, and they continued to share their Paris residence.[34]

Vigée-LeBrun spent two weeks visiting Madame de Staël at Coppet, where she lived in exile from Bonaparte's government. The daughter of Louis XVI's finance minister, Jacques Necker, Madame de Staël was a popular and outspoken writer. Vigée-LeBrun painted an imposing portrait of her as Corinne, which had been the title of de Staël's most recent novel, *Corine ou l'Italie.* Moving on to Geneva, Chamonix, and Vevey, where she painted a number of landscapes, Vigée-LeBrun luxuriated in the beauties of nature and the solitude she found in Switzerland.[35]

Following her return to Paris in December 1809, Vigée-LeBrun purchased a large house in the village of Louveciennes on the route between Versailles and Paris. Henceforth, she would pass her springs and summers there near Marly-le-Roi, where she had painted the ill-fated Madame du Barry's portrait before the revolution. She noted that du Barry's home had been stripped of everything, even the locks and bronzes from the fireplaces, while at Marly, Sceaux, Belle-Vue, and other places, everything had been destroyed down to the foundations.[36]

During the fall and winter months, Vigée-LeBrun led an active life in Paris, where she continued to paint portraits, and she exhibited works at the Salon in 1817 and 1824. Her 1787 painting of "Marie Antoinette and her Children," which had been placed in "one of Versailles' darkest corners" during the Empire, attracted favorable attention at the Salon of 1817. According to her memoir, many visitors had come to see the famous portrait during Napoleon's reign, but they were only allowed to see it if they paid a fee. Altogether, following her return to Paris in 1802, Vigée-LeBrun listed sixty works that she had completed by the time she wrote her memoirs in 1835–1837.[37]

Vigée-LeBrun's memoir, *Souvenirs*, served as the "authorized" version of a life that she feared others might choose to write about in less flattering terms. She presented herself as a beautiful woman of somewhat humble origins, endowed with great artistic talent, who had counted among her patrons the French royal family and the courts of Europe, and had been honored by the great academies of art.[38] In addition to serving as a sympathetic chronicle of an exceptional woman's life, the three volumes of *Souvenirs* provide a valuable record of the interaction between art and patronage in the late eighteenth and early nineteenth centuries. Her recollections of the social and cultural life in Paris before the revolution offer fascinating, if sometimes biased, accounts of the period. Vigée-LeBrun wrote in "bits and pieces" with an apparent disregard for the rules of grammar and spelling. She did not always date events accurately; rather, she wrote about her experiences as she recalled them, and not in chronological order. Her writing style, however, is engaging and filled with detailed and lively visual descriptions of people and places.[39] While a 1989 English translation makes *Souvenirs* available to more readers, it fails to capture the particular brightness of the author's style.[40]

Of the approximately eight hundred works painted by Vigée-LeBrun, ninety-eight to one hundred of them were exhibited in Paris between 1774 and 1824, the date of her last Salon exhibition. Her prolific output, especially before the period of exile from 1789 to 1801, ensured that she would be honored and remembered as an accomplished artist. A debilitating stroke in 1841 led to her death, at the age of eighty-seven, in her Paris apartment on 29 March 1842. Buried in the old cemetery of Louveciennes, her grave is marked by an appropriate stone showing a relief carving of a palette and brushes, as she had requested in her will. A white ceramic, heart-shaped plaque inscribed "Souvenir" is affixed to the gravestone. Her life, as she wrote in the last chapter of *Souvenirs*, had been "nomadic but peaceful, hard-working but honorable."[41]

Jean-Baptiste Pierre LeBrun had died years earlier in 1813, but his last years had been productive as well. From the time that Dominique Vivant-Denon had dismissed him from his position at the national museum in 1802, LeBrun had focused on his business as an art dealer and on building up private collections. Always adept at aligning himself with the government in power, in an 1810 publication, *Choix des Tableaux*, he praised the relationship between royalty and artists, citing especially the influence of "Napoleon le Grand," who had done so much for the arts during his reign. [42]

LeBrun's travels in Spain in 1807 and 1808 had presented fresh opportunities for him to discover great paintings by Velasquez, Murillo, and others, many of which he brought back to France. The illustrated sales catalog that he produced to accompany the exhibition of Spanish masters contained "some of the first illustrations of the work of these artists outside their native country," according to the late art historian, Francis Haskell. LeBrun also noted the work of Goya, among the earliest references to that Spanish artist. [43]

Several of the Spanish masters' works were included among those that LeBrun offered for sale in 1810. This sale over a five-day period netted over 183,000 francs. LeBrun held another sale in 1811 featuring recent acquisitions from Flanders, Switzerland, and Holland. Although he held only twenty-one sales between 1804 and 1813, the quality of the featured works remained high and continued to attract amateurs and collectors, but not foreign dealers. [44]

Not only had the commercial center shifted from Paris to London between 1804 and 1813, but Napoleon's Continental blockade, intended to break the British economy, had also interfered significantly with commerce between Great Britain and France. LeBrun's extensive commercial correspondence for the period provides evidence of the difficulties that he encountered when he attempted to sell paintings in Great Britain. He never seemed to receive the prices to which he felt entitled, and he regretted the disappearance of the pre-revolutionary style of conducting business "between gentlemen." [45] The apparent success of LeBrun's public sales stands in contrast to his difficulties negotiating in the private art market during the Continental blockade.

In 1807 LeBrun, ever in need of funds, allowed his financially solvent former wife to settle many of his debts, for which she received mortgages on his real properties and bought from him the Hôtel de Lubert, including its outbuildings and gardens. Vigée-LeBrun claimed in her memoir that, while she had not been close to her former husband for some time, she was "sorely affected by his death." When LeBrun died in August 1813, he left his townhouse on the rue du Gros Chênet to their only child, Julie. She would die from pneumonia only six years later. [46] Had LeBrun lived into the next decade, there is little doubt that he would have cheered the return of the Bourbons to the throne, relating to his former patrons as he had before the revolution.

His friend Jacques-Louis David, however, had chosen to go into exile in Brussels during the Bourbon Restoration. David remained loyal to Napoleon, a leader whom he regarded as comparable to those of antiquity, both in physical beauty (as a young man) and in military skill. As the revolution's leading artist and as an active propagandist and participant in its government, David had captured the dramatic events of the period, and he would continue to do so under the First Empire. His often-reproduced depiction of "Napoleon Crossing the Alps at the Grande Saint Bernard" (1800) has come to represent the leader of French forces at the zenith of his military career. David had skillfully mingled myth with reality to achieve a stunning composition. The painting, showing a dignified Napoleon on his rearing horse, captured the heroic elements of the battle of 20 May 1800, which led to the reconquest of northern Italy. As an added touch of grandeur, the name "Bonaparte" appeared inscribed next to those of Charlemagne and Hannibal on the rocks beneath the horse's hooves. David's well-known coronation scene, "Tableau du Sacre" (1807), also contributed to the royal aspect of Napoleon's reign, and by the emperor's order it was exhibited at the national museum from February to March 1808. David had been commissioned by Napoleon to "glorify his reign," and he had succeeded admirably. Following the final defeat of Napoleon by the Allied forces in 1815, David chose exile rather than accepting a pardon from the Bourbons.[47] In Brussels he continued to paint portraits of former revolutionaries and Bonapartists who were also in exile, and to produce mythological works.[48] Perhaps David's best portraits from this period were those of his close friends, Mr. and Mme. Ramel de Nogaret (1820), now in private collections. Following Napoleon's defeat, Nogaret, a former deputy, and his wife had moved to Brussels, where they continued their friendship with David. When the artist died in 1825, Ramel de Nogaret gave the funeral oration and secured a burial plot for David and his family in Brussels. The Bourbon government had refused permission to inter his body on French soil.[49] A Bonapartist to the end, it is unlikely that David would have agreed with the Bourbon kings about anything, although he might have preferred to rest in his native land.

Marguerite Gérard, known for her nonpolitical genre scenes, also painted at least one portrait of Napoléon, "La Clémence de Napoléon à Mme. Hatzfeld à Berlin," exhibited at the Salon of 1808. Her one documented history painting shows the emperor favorably in a chivalrous pose. The Empress Josephine was so taken by this *scène galante* that she persuaded the emperor to buy the painting for her private collection at Malmaison.[50] Gérard's scenes of mothers and children were popular under the First Empire, fitting in well with the dominant philosophical mood after the revolution. Napoleon's Civil Code of 1804 had subordinated women to male dominance, instructing them to be good mothers and remain at home. In 1804 Gérard exhibited eight paintings at the Salon and was awarded a gold medal worth 500 francs for her outstanding achievement in genre painting.[51]

Gérard continued to paint and exhibit her works at the Salon through 1824, but a combination of unflattering reviews and an increasingly busy role as the family matriarch contributed finally to her retirement as an artist. Official records of her business transactions as an independent unmarried woman indicate that she had succeeded financially as well as artistically. She had bought and sold houses with the Fragonards and had loaned money to a number of persons, including several aristocrats. The documents of purchases and sales of land and/or lodgings date from 1797, when Gérard, Fragonard, and his wife (Gérard's sister) bought a house for 5,000 livres in Evry-Petit-Bourg (Seine). Gérard retained ownership while the Fragonards collected interest. Gérard sold the house for a profit in 1824.[52]

By the time of her death in 1837 at the age of seventy-six, in her apartment on the rue Neuve de Petits-Champs in Paris, Gérard's estate was valued at over 51,000 francs, excluding her personal possessions, which were listed in a special inventory that apparently has been lost. Her biographer, Wells-Robertson, wrote that Gérard's jewelry, furnishings, and paintings "must have been considerable," because Gérard's heirs had commissioned the lost inventory, and also because the artist had referred to diamonds in her last will and testament (1826). Her estate was divided between her nephew, Alexandre-Evariste Fragonard, and her brother, Henri Gérard.[53]

Gérard's artistic production has been somewhat difficult to ascertain, owing to a lack of attribution as well as the misattribution of some works, and incomplete information about the contents of private collections. Her biographer lists 148 works with reproductions, 222 without reproductions, and 149 disputed works and misattributions, for a total of 519.[54]

If Elisabeth Vigée-LeBrun had lived a more glamorous life as a celebrated artist in Paris and at the courts of Europe during her exile, Marguerite Gérard had also succeeded as an artist, albeit on a much quieter level. They had both achieved financial security, however, during a period when most women were dependent upon the male members of their families for support. Both had also managed to survive the chaos of the revolution, living well into old age, which was not a minor accomplishment for those of their generation.

NOTES

1. Honoré Riouffe, *Mémoires d'un Détenu, pour servir à l'histoire de la tyrannie de Robespierre* (2nd ed., revue et augmentée) (Paris: De l'Imprimerie d'Anjubault, L'An III de la Republique Française).

2. Riouffe, *Mémoires d'un Détenu*, 15–21, 25, 36–39, 42–52.

3. Riouffe, *Mémoires d'un Détenu*, 53–55.

4. Riouffe, *Mémoires d'un Détenu*, 56n1.

5. Riouffe, *Mémoires d'un Détenu*, 57–61.

6. Riouffe, *Mémoires d'un Détenu*, 62–65.

7. Riouffe, *Mémoires d'un Détenu*, 65–70.

8. Riouffe, *Mémoires d'un Détenu*, 71–78.

9. Riouffe, *Mémoires d'un Détenu*, 79, 83–84, 86–88, 94.

10. Riouffe, *Mémoires d'un Détenu*, 90–92.

11. Riouffe, *Mémoires d'un Détenu*, 132, 102, 107–11.

12. Riouffe, *Mémoires d'un Détenu*, 113–17.

13. Riouffe, *Mémoires d'un Détenu*, 119–22.

14. Riouffe, *Mémoires d'un Détenu*, 126–32.

15. Riouffe, *Mémoires d'un Détenu*, 140–49.

16. Riouffe, *Mémoires d'un Détenu*, 150–58.

17. Riouffe, *Mémoires d'un Détenu*, 158–63.

18. Riouffe, *Mémoires d'un Détenu*, 164–68.

19. Riouffe, *Mémoires d'un Détenu*, 169–70. The stanzas comprise pages 171–77 of his memoir.

20. Riouffe, *Mémoires d'un Détenu*, 178–88.

21. Riouffe, *Mémoires d'un Détenu*, 191–92; Mme. Roland's defense, 199–214.

22. Eloise Ellery, *Brissot de Warville: A Study in the History of the French Revolution* (Boston and New York: Houghton Mifflin, 1915; reprint New York: Burt Franklin, 1970), 406 ("Procès-verbal de la Convention, Oct. 3, 1795").

23. Ellery, *Brissot de Warville*, 407 ("Résolution du conseil des Cinq-Cents, 7 floréal, An IV").

24. C. A. Dauban, ed., *Mémoires Inédits de Pétion et Mémoires de Buzot & de Barbaroux, accompagnés de Notes Inédites de Buzot et de nombreux documents inédits sur Barbaroux, Buzot, Brissot, etc.* (Paris: Henri Plon, 1866), lxx–lxxiii, xlix.

25. Ellery, *Brissot de Warville*, 405–6. The contents included furniture and other household furnishings, books, clothing, and wine.

26. Ellery, *Brissot de Warville*, 407–11. See also *Papiers de Roland II*, N. A. F. 9534, f. 392 (Paris: Bibliothèque Nationale, Dept. des Manuscrits).

27. Dauban, *Mémoires Inédits*, 510–12. The "last letters" of the fugitives and Troquart's petition were published in *Le Moniteur*, 24 Messidor An III (12 July 1795).

28. Paul R. Hanson, *The Jacobin Republic Under Fire: The Federalist Revolt in the French Revolution* (University Park: Pennsylvania State University Press, 2003), 233.

29. John Rivers, *Louvet: Revolutionist & Romance-Writer* (London: Hurst and Blackett, Ltd., Paternoster House, E. C., 1910), 325–26.

30. Rivers, *Louvet*, 343–47.

31. Elisabeth Louise Vigée-LeBrun, *Souvenirs*, 3 vols. (Paris: Librairie de H. Fournier, 1835–1837), III: 133–38.

32. Vigée-LeBrun, *Souvenirs*, III: 31–32; Joseph Baillio, *Elisabeth Vigée-LeBrun 1755–1842* exhibition catalogue, Kimbell Art Museum (Fort Worth, Tex.: Kimbell Art Museum, 1982), 15.

33. Vigée-LeBrun, *Souvenirs*, III: 204, 155–215, 178–80.

34. Baillio, *Elisabeth Vigée-LeBrun*, 15.

35. Charles Nicoullaud, ed., *Memoirs of the Countess de Boigne, 1781–1814* (New York: Charles Scribner's Sons, 1908), 239; Mary D. Sheriff, *The Exceptional Woman: Elisabeth Vigée-LeBrun and the Cultural Politics of Art* (Chicago: University of Chicago Press, 1996), 259; Vigée-LeBrun, *Souvenirs*, III: 25l, 262.

36. Vigée-LeBrun, *Souvenirs*, III: 298–99.

37. Vigée-LeBrun, *Souvenirs*, III: 316–17; Baillio, *Elisabeth Vigée-LeBrun*, 19.

38. Baillio, *Elisabeth Vigée-LeBrun*, 129–30.

39. Baillio, *Elisabeth Vigée-LeBrun*, 130.

40. See Sian Evans, *The Memoirs of Elisabeth Vigée-LeBrun* (Bloomington: Indiana University Press, 1989).

41. Baillio, *Elisabeth Vigée-LeBrun*, 16; Ann S. Harris and Linda Nochlin, *Women Artists 1550–1950* exhibition catalogue, Los Angeles Museum of Art (New York: Alfred A. Knopf, 1976), 191. See also *Papiers Tripier le Franc*, Carton 52, Dossier II, in Bibliothèque Doucet, Paris. Vigée-LeBrun's home in Louveciennes was left to her niece, Caroline Rivière. Vigée-LeBrun's daughter Julie had died in 1819 at the age of thirty-nine.

42. Jean-Baptiste Pierre LeBrun, *Choix des tableaux les plus capitaux de la rare et précieuse collection recueillie dans l'Espagne et dans l'Italie, par M. LeBrun dans les années 1807 et 1808* (Paris, 1810), Discours Préliminaire, ix–x.

43. Francis Haskell, *Rediscoveries in Art: Some Aspects of Taste, Fashion and Collecting in England and France*, the Wrightsman Lectures, New York University, Institute of Fine Arts (London: Phaidon Press, Ltd., 1976), 22.

44. Jean-Baptiste Pierre LeBrun, *Recueil de gravures au trait, à l'eau-forte et ombrées, d'après un choix de tableaux de toutes les écoles recueillis dans un voyage fait en Espagne, au midi de la France et en Italie dans les Années 1807 et 1808 par M. LeBrun, peintre*, 2 tomes (Paris: Imprimerie Didot jeune, 1809), Bibliothèque Doucet, 8 F1293 (VII 422); Gilberte Emile-Mâle, "Jean-Baptiste Pierre LeBrun (1748–1813): Son Rôle dans l'Histoire de la Restauration des Tableaux du Louvre," *Paris et Île-de-France 8* (Paris, 1956): 371–417.

45. *Papiers Tripier le Franc*, Documents Autographes, Carton 52, Bibliothèque Doucet; Colin B. Bailey, "LeBrun et le commerce d'art pendant le Blocus continental," *Revue de l'Art 63* (1984): 35–46.

46. Baillio, *Elisabeth Vigée-LeBrun*, 15; Vigée-LeBrun, *Souvenirs*, III: 329; *Papiers Tripier le Franc*, Carton 51, nos. 27342 and 27395-27455, Bibliothèque Doucet.

47. Alan Wintermute, *The French Portrait 1550–1850* exhibition catalogue Colnaghi, New York, January 10–February 10, 1996 (New York: Colnaghi, 1996), 113.

48. Warren Roberts, *Jacques-Louis David, Revolutionary Artist* (Chapel Hill: University of North Carolina Press, 1989), 6–7.

49. Wintermute, *The French Portrait*, 76–77. Ramel de Nogaret, who had served as a deputy in the Constituent Assembly, the National Convention, and the Directory, is credited with the introduction of the franc in the French fiscal system.

50. Sally Wells-Robertson, *Marguerite Gérard 1761–1837*, 4 vols. (doctoral dissertation, New York University, 1978), vol. I, part 1: 208.

51. Wells-Robertson, *Marguerite Gérard*, vol. I, part 1: 269.

52. Wells-Robertson, *Marguerite Gérard*, vol. I, part 1: 291, 257, 267, 268, 271, 273 (listed in the Minutier Central, Archives Nationales, Paris).

53. Wells-Robertson, *Marguerite Gérard*, vol. I, part 1: 274 (Archives de la Seine, Paris). Additional papers of Marguerite Gérard and the Fragonard family are located in the Archives du Musée Fragonard, Grasse.

54. Wells-Robertson, *Marguerite Gérard*, vol. II, part 1: 719–933; vol. II, part 2: 934–98, 999–1043.

Conclusion

The experience of exile led to both physical and emotional dislocation, sadness at loss of the familiar, and anxiety produced by belonging to neither the lost world of the Ancien Régime or to the new and confusing world that had been produced by the revolution. Yet even those who had not left France during that period shared the sense of disorientation, of being suspended on a bridge across time that led to a place yet to be determined. While there existed the promise and excitement of a better, more equitable society, there also existed the discomfort of what the historian Peter Fritzsche has referred to as being "stranded in the present."[1]

As regime changes produced new political outcasts, the experiences of exile and dislocation would be felt by succeeding generations throughout the nineteenth century.[2] Yet the initial disruption between 1789 and 1794, the replacement of the centuries-old monarchy by a republic, marks the first and most profound of such changes. The acceleration of time resulting from the dramatic unfolding of events following the fall of the Bastille only increased the sense of anxiety felt by the inhabitants of France, especially in Paris. Even in 1788 the city could be "experienced as a series of overlapping temporalities," ranging from that of the church to the marketplace and the salon; thus Paris already existed as a center of change before the revolution.[3]

The "outpouring of voices," both oral and written, that had resulted from the end of pre-publication censorship in the summer of 1788 increased markedly in 1789, when 184 new journals appeared, many of them short-lived. By 1790 Gouverneur Morris reported that Paris seemed to be "in a sort of whirlwind which turns [one] round so fast that one can see nothing . . . as all Men and Things are in the same vertiginous Situation, you can neither fix yourself nor your object for regular examination."[4]

With everyone writing or talking, often all at the same time, the revolutionary government in 1792 sought to impose a sense of order by restoring some form of censorship. The increasing radicalization of the revolution in 1793–1794 led to even stricter government control of free speech as well as more severe penalties for those who disobeyed. The Paris Commune banned counter-revolutionary newspapers in 1792, and the National Convention imposed further restrictions in 1793. By 1794 the exhilarating sense of freedom experienced and manifested in the early years of the revolution had been replaced by the legal repression of the

Terror, and by 1800, only about a dozen newspapers out of the seventy-three that had existed earlier were still being published.[5]

The fervent hopes for regeneration promised by the early leaders of the revolution had led instead to the loss of liberty and the executions of thousands of French citizens, even some once praised as patriots. Yet the Terror of 1793–1794 need not be seen as an inherent part of the French Revolution; rather, it had evolved from the desperation of the Jacobin leaders to preserve the Republic from what they perceived as enemies within (the monarchy and the Girondins) and enemies outside France (the émigrés and other European powers). The violent excesses of the period were a direct result of the bitter factional divisions that could not be resolved within the chambers of the National Convention. Thus, former friends and associates who had sometimes served together in the Constituent or Legislative Assemblies became relentless enemies, culminating in the expulsion of the Girondin deputies from the Convention in May/June 1793.

Yet only extreme idealists such as Jacques-Pierre Brissot could have actually believed that the French Revolution would follow the American example. Indeed, even Brissot only believed it initially, before he had become a leader of the Girondins. As has often been noted, the revolutionary circumstances in the American colonies were vastly different than those in France. Representative government had been established long before America's break with England and a sense of civic responsibility and domestic order had developed during the century preceding the American Revolution. Consequently, Americans were better prepared for self-government than the French, who had lived under an absolute monarchy for centuries and had not been adequately educated for the demands of republican government. The missing ingredient was time, as Gouverneur Morris expressed so clearly in a diary entry from 1796:

> In effect, Time is needed to bring forward Slaves to the Enjoyment of Liberty. Time. Time. Education. But what is Education? It is not Learning. It is more the Effect of Society on the Habits and Principles of each Individual, forming him at an early Period of Life to act afterwards the Part of a good Citizen and contribute in his turn to the Formation of others. Hence it results that the Progress towards Freedom must be slow and can only be completed in the Course of several Generations. The French Nation jumped at once from a mild Monarchy to a wild Anarchy and are now in Subjection to Men whom they despise.[6]

Although not nearly as eloquently, Jacques Necker had written as early as 1792, "It would be a great fallacy to imagine that liberty, equality, and all our other new institutions will make us similar to Americans."[7] Indeed, it would take time, almost one hundred years, before France would be able to establish a stable republic.

The excitement and enthusiasm of 1789 were soon replaced by a realization of the myriad problems facing the revolutionary government. By 1791 Brissot was expressing doubts that the French people were actually ready for the blessings of liberty. In the preface to his book about his travels in the United States, he had written, "We have won our liberty. We have, therefore, no need to learn from Americans how to attain this blessing; but we do have to learn from them the secret of preserving it."[8] The lack of consensus among the deputies, which increased after the execution of Louis XVI in January 1793, underscored the divergent views of how best to govern France. While the Girondins, who found more support in the provinces than in Paris, favored a republic based on the rule of law supported by moral principles, the Jacobins embraced popular sovereignty, the will of the people, as a means to legitimize the republican government and its policies. Brissot, Buzot, and other Girondin leaders did not share such faith in the wisdom of "the people," especially those in Paris, fearing that political power in their hands would lead to violence. Unfortunately, their fears would be realized, as the Paris Commune and the political sections strongly supported Robespierre and his associates in 1793 and early 1794. The Jacobins were better organized and more unified in their goals than the Girondins, which gave them a decided advantage as the revolution escalated.

Another matter that caused serious dissension among the deputies was the decision to go to war against those who were harboring émigrés. Brissot's articles in the *Patriote Français* provide evidence of his passionate calls for war against Austria to prevent an invasion of France by émigré and royalist forces. His role in involving France in costly European wars is obvious but, according to his memoir, he never thought of himself as anything but a selfless patriot working to create a better world for all French citizens.[9] Robespierre, however, refuted Brissot and argued against going to war, pointing out that France was not America, and therefore "America's example, as an argument for our success, is worthless, because the circumstances are different."[10] Where Brissot perceived war as a preventive measure, Robespierre and the Jacobins feared that France's involvement in war would detract from the need to consolidate the gains of the revolution.

It is important to remember that there were no obvious or well-established guideposts for the deputies to follow in the new world of republican France. They found themselves besieged on all sides as events accelerated at such a pace that they had little time to pause and consider the most judicious course to follow. Revolutions chart their own courses. People found it difficult to internalize the rapid succession of changes; consequently, they experienced a sort of mental and emotional vertigo. As Ken Alder phrased it in a recent book, "The revolution had broken time, reset the clocks, and torn down the calendars."[11]

If those who remained in France experienced confusion and discomfort, that was no less true for those who had sought safety elsewhere. Many who had hoped to wait out the revolution in places outside the French borders found that they were not always welcome. French émigrés moved from town to town as their hosts grew impatient with their presence, and as the French armies invaded Belgium, the Austrian Netherlands, Italy, and the German states. If the émigrés were found, they were subject to arrest. "Our fate," mourned one French count who had briefly found refuge in Spa, "is to be ceaselessly victims of events."[12] Few of the émigrés in Europe were as fortunate as Elisabeth Vigée-LeBrun, who, because her portraits were highly prized, could afford to settle for varying periods at foreign courts. Many émigrés experienced financial as well as emotional stress as they moved around Europe, and the French government's confiscation of their properties only added to their distress. The nobles whose property had been sold by the government after 1792 did not receive recompense until 1825, when they were awarded annual pensions that hardly replaced all that they had lost.[13] And even after they had returned home, many émigrés reported that they did not feel "at home"; too much had changed in their absence, as noted in memoirs by Vigée-LeBrun and others who had endured a period of exile.

The émigrés who had chosen refuge in the United States, although safer in many respects, nevertheless faced challenges that many found difficult, if not downright unpleasant. This was especially true for those who had purchased land in the Ohio Valley. Not only did they discover that they did not hold the titles to their lands, thanks to the machinations of the Scioto Company, but they also found that their wilderness homes had not been accurately described in the land company's *Prospectus*. Nevertheless, a number of them managed to make their homes in the Ohio Valley and adapted to frontier conditions. Others sought the society of their compatriots in cities of the Northeast, while some even chose to return to France. Much depended on their reasons for coming to the United States. Those seeking employment and better lives for their children determined to make a success of their new lives. Others, like the aristocrats who were members of "the 24," were less motivated to remain.[14]

While the original settlers of Gallipolis experienced many hardships because they simply were not prepared for life on the American frontier, the settlement itself did manage to survive, unlike several other French attempts during the period from 1789 to 1815. A contemporary French historian, Jocelyne Moreau-Zanelli, who has written the most recent account of French settlement in Ohio, considers the settlement of Gallipolis a success despite the "collusion and corruption" of the epoch and the misrepresentations of the Scioto Company. In the conclusion to her book, she cites the two "tenacious convictions" that predominated at the end of the eighteenth century: that the uninhabited American west was a possible source of profits for speculators, and that a "golden age" awaited in the virgin wilderness of America. These commonly held beliefs motivated the land speculators as well as the French émigrés seeking a better life in America.[15]

Those émigrés who had planned only a temporary exile in the United States, such as Talleyrand and Madame de la Tour du Pin, made the best of their temporary home, especially Madame de la Tour du Pin, who according to her memoir rather enjoyed her adventures as a farmer's wife, albeit a prosperous one. Finding solace in the company of their countrymen, the group of émigrés in the northeastern United States enjoyed a fairly comfortable existence, even if some were anxious to return to France just as soon as conditions allowed.

As for those who remained in France, some were able to take advantage of new opportunities while simultaneously practicing their chosen professions. Jean-Baptiste Pierre LeBrun, whose expertise in the art world was well established by 1789, simply changed his political position to suit the times. While his exiled wife was occupied with painting portraits at the courts of Europe (and sending money home to help her husband), LeBrun worked to preserve their property and his art gallery in Paris. His friendship with the revolutionary artist Jacques-Louis David led to an important position in the national museum, where LeBrun dealt with the acquisition, reparation, and exhibition of confiscated artworks between 1794 and 1802. He also continued to engage in commercial transactions, buying and selling works for his gallery and for private collectors. In addition, he found time to write and publish a number of works about the museum and to compile exhibition catalogs.

David, an ardent Jacobin, not only created some of the most memorable paintings of the period but also served as a deputy in the National Convention. His fame only increased during the reign of Napoleon as he produced some suitably iconic portraits of the emperor. Other artists, such as Marguerite Gérard, Adélaide Labile-Guiard, and Anne Vallayer-Coster, also continued to pursue their artistic careers successfully throughout the revolution.

The writers discussed in this book did not fare as well, primarily because they insisted on speaking their minds when it was not safe to do so. Both the poet André Chénier, who earlier had been David's friend, and Sébastien Chamfort, the aphorist and first co-director of the national library, might have survived if they had been less outspoken. While Chénier allied himself with neither faction, he made serious enemies with his written attacks on government figures. As for Chamfort, he enjoyed the friendship of a number of the Girondins, the Rolands among them, and made no secret of his sympathies for them, even cheering openly on the occasion of Marat's assassination by Charlotte Corday. Both Chénier and Chamfort paid for their honesty with their lives.[16]

The same might be said of the Girondin deputies who perished during the Terror, both those who remained in Paris following their expulsion from the Convention in May/June 1793 and those fugitives who fled to other parts of France. It is tempting to imagine what might have resulted had those fugitives crossed over from Brittany into England instead of sailing down to the Bordeaux area. Their memoirs, written on the run or in prison, bear witness to their perceptions of events and amount to what they hoped would be a posthumous vindication of their actions.

The fugitives, labeled as traitors and federalists by the radical government, deplored the willingness of "the people" to believe the Jacobin propaganda, even as they admitted their lack of faith in the wisdom of ordinary citizens. François Buzot criticized the naiveté of the people and the "imbecility" of the masses under a corrupt government. Jérôme Pétion, once the mayor of Paris, noted that fear "freezes the courage of weak men" and blamed the Parisians for "elevating the brigands who have taken over our city." In his prison memoir Jacques-Pierre Brissot regretted that he had sacrificed so much time engaged in political matters, both as a newspaper editor and as a deputy, while his family had suffered from poverty and neglect.[17] Unlike the Jacobins, who used popular sovereignty to strengthen their power base, the Girondins lacked the popular support needed to rally citizens in the provinces to join them in their revolt against the central government in Paris.

Those Girondins imprisoned in Paris had been declared as guilty as those who had fled, because all had acted against the policies of the government. "For the revolutionary, all opposition is necessarily counter-revolutionary," according to the radical government; thus, the twenty-one Girondin prisoners were judged guilty and executed on 31 October 1793. Despite the fact that the Girondins had acted more as individuals than as a political party, the government had decided that if all of them "could be accused as conspirators, all could be convicted on a single capital charge."[18] Madame Roland, also accused of conspiracy, would follow them only a few days later, while the fugitives would die, either by their own hands or by execution, in June 1794.

A friend of the Girondins, the journalist Honoré Riouffe, imprisoned from October 1793 to July 1794, has left a poignant account of life inside a prison during the Terror. Riouffe felt fortunate to have survived, but he could not forget the many people he had witnessed going to their deaths every day. In effect, he wrote that he remained haunted by their presence. After he was released from prison following Robespierre's downfall, Riouffe regretted that those on the "outside" showed no desire to learn about his experiences, nor could they ever understand what he had endured.[19]

If Riouffe found himself not only sad but also misunderstood following his release, he was not alone in feeling somewhat disoriented by his recent experiences. The Thermidorian Reaction of 1794–1795 included the

establishment of a less authoritarian government controlled by the National Convention, which set about dismantling the draconian measures
enacted under the Terror. Those who had been repressed soon rejoiced in
their newfound freedom, celebrating with balls and street parties. At the
"Victims' Balls," the participants who had lost relatives to the guillotine
sported red ribbons around their necks. The *Incroyables* ("Gilded Youth")
and their female counterparts, the *Marveilleuses* ("Wonderfuls"), took
over the streets and attacked former Terrorists. The reaction in the provinces followed more slowly. Some former Jacobin officials were imprisoned or killed, while Catholic groups in the rural areas of the south
sought vengeance during a "White Terror."[20]

Once again French citizens found themselves living in a new world,
neither that of the Ancien Régime nor that of the revolution. Economic
problems increased due to weather conditions and hoarding, aggravated
by the falling value of the *assignats*; the cost of food in April 1795 had
risen to eight times what it had been in 1790. Meanwhile, the government, wary of centralizing power, worked to produce a new constitution
that provided for the separation of powers. The new government, known
as the Directory, featured a bicameral legislature composed of the Council of Elders and the Council of Five Hundred. A Directory of five men,
selected by the Council of Elders from a list of names drawn up by the
Council of Five Hundred, served as the executive branch. Although the
new government was an improvement, the Constitution of the Year III
(1795) had not provided the means by which the legislative and executive
branches could resolve their disagreements; this situation would not encourage the orderly transfer of power.[21]

Paris in 1797 had lost one-fifth of its population to the revolution,
wars, and emigration. Yet despite these losses, those who visited the
capital city noticed an "air of gaiety." In addition to the fancy balls given
by aristocrats and the street dances, cabarets also offered music and dancing. Outside activities including puppet shows competed with the theaters to entertain the public; fourteen of the twenty-three theaters in Paris
featured a play every night. Once again both written and spoken words
proliferated as France looked forward to a new century. "Three poets had
gone to the guillotine—Fabre d'Eglantine, Jean-Antoine Roucher, and
André Chénier—but others were taking their places in an explosion of
works in verse."[22]

The emergence of Napoleon Bonaparte, first as consul and then as
emperor, ensured that the first years of the nineteenth century would be
more orderly than the previous decade, but peace would prove elusive
until his forced abdication in 1815. By that time the French people, exhausted by twenty-six years of revolution and war, were more than ready
for peace even if it meant a return to Bourbon rule. Some, such as Vigée-
LeBrun, welcomed their return to power, while others, including David,
chose exile. At the very least, the Bourbon Restoration provided an op-

portunity for the French to catch their collective breaths and reflect on the significance of what they had experienced.

Memoirs, often written during the chaotic years of the revolution, would emerge throughout the nineteenth century, offering firsthand accounts of the causes of the upheaval that began in 1789. The appearance of these memoirs was accompanied by efforts to preserve documents from the revolutionary period, especially during more liberal regimes. Memory and history existed within a political context during the nineteenth century and could be manipulated to serve a particular purpose at a specified time. Therefore, contemporary views of the past changed according to the government in power at the time. For example, during more liberal periods in 1830 and 1848, the government worked to reintegrate the history of the 1789 revolution into the official national history, while under the Second Empire there was less interest in doing so. Both the late July Monarchy and the early Second Empire came into power following popular revolutions. The so-called Liberal Empire of 1869 made efforts to compromise between republicanism and authoritarianism, but its promise was cut short by the Franco-Prussian War of 1870 and the Commune of 1871. Following the French defeat in 1870, many memoirs of the Napoleonic period were published in an effort to recall more glorious times in the nation's history.

Finally, under the government of the Third Republic, which followed the 1870 debacle, the papers and documents from the 1790s received new attention "as the revolutionary legacy became a treasure to be explored" rather than a period to be suppressed. In early 1866 the Sorbonne had established its first chair in the history of the revolution, and with the centennial celebration of the revolution in 1889, more collections of revolution-era papers began to appear.[23] Under the Third Republic the French Revolution had assumed its rightful place in the national history, and there it would remain under succeeding republics.

The great revolution may have ended officially in 1794, but it had taken eighty-two long years before the hopes of the early leaders could be realized in the establishment of a stable republic. It had taken time. As Gouverneur Morris had written so presciently in 1796, "In effect, Time is needed to bring forward Slaves to the Enjoyment of Liberty. Time. Time. Education."[24]

NOTES

1. Peter Fritzsche, *Stranded in the Present: Modern Time and the Melancholy of History* (Cambridge, Mass.: Harvard University Press, 2004).

2. Sylvie Aprile, *La siècle des exilés: Bannis et proscrits de 1789 à la Commune* (Paris: CNRS Éditions, 2010).

3. Daniel Roche, *France in the Enlightenment*, trans. Arthur Goldhammer (Cambridge, Mass./London: Harvard University Press, 1998), 646.

4. See Sophia Rosenfeld, "On Being Heard: A Case for Paying Attention to the Historical Ear," in AHR Forum, *American Historical Review* 116, no. 2 (April 2011): 316–34; Caroline Moorehead, *Dancing to the Precipice: Lucie de la Tour du Pin and the French Revolution* (London: Chatto & Windus, 2009), 131.

5. Moorehead, *Dancing to the Precipice*, 277–78.

6. William Howard Adams, *Gouverneur Morris: An Independent Life* (New Haven, Conn.: Yale University Press, 2003), 250.

7. Durand Echeverria, *Mirage in the West: A History of the French Image of American Society to 1815* (New York: Octagon Books, 1966), 212. He quotes from Jacques Necker, *Du pouvoir exécutif dans les grands états* (Paris, 1792), II, 7.

8. J.-P. Brissot de Warville, *New Travels in the United States of America, 1788*, trans. Mara Soceanu Vamos and Durand Echeverria (Cambridge, Mass.: Belknap Press of Harvard University Press, 1964), xi.

9. See Cl. Perroud, ed., *J.-P. Brissot, Mémoires* (Paris: Librairie Alphonse Picard & Fils, 1910).

10. Eloise Ellery, *Brissot de Warville: A Study in the History of the French Revolution* (Boston and New York: Houghton Mifflin, 1915; reprint New York: Burt Franklin, 1970), 238 ("Discours de Maximilien Robespierre sur la guerre, Jan. 2, 1792").

11. Ken Alder, *The Measure of All Things: The Seven-Year Odyssey that Transformed the World* (London: Abacus, 2004), 204.

12. Moorehead, *Dancing to the Precipice*, 157.

13. Peter Fritzsche, "Specters of History: On Nostalgia, Exile, and Modernity," in *American Historical Review* 106, no. 5 (December 2001): 1587–1618.

14. See chapter 3 for a description of the Scioto Company and the settlement of Gallipolis.

15. Jocelyne Moreau-Zanelli, *Gallipolis: Histoire d'un Mirage Américain au XVIII Siècle* (Paris and Montreal: L'Harmattan, 2000), 256–57, 381–84, 411, 420.

16. See chapter 4 for a discussion of several artists and writers during the revolutionary period. See also Bette W. Oliver, *From Royal to National: The Louvre Museum and the Bibliothèque Nationale* (Lanham, Md.: Lexington Books, 2007).

17. F.-L.-N. Buzot, *Mémoires de Buzot*, N. A. F. 1730, 75; Jérôme Pétion, *Mémoires de Jérôme Pétion*, N. A. F. 1730, 95–96 (Paris: Bibliothèque Nationale, Dept. des Manuscrits); Cl. Perroud, ed., *J.-P. Brissot, Mémoires*, II: 262–71.

18. M. J. Sydenham, *The Girondins* (London: University of London, Athlone Press, 1961), 27–30.

19. Honoré Riouffe, *Mémoires d'un Détenu, pour servir à l'histoire de la tyrannie de Robespierre* (2nd ed., revue et augmentée) (Paris: De l'Imprimerie d'Anjubault, L'An III de la Republique Française).

20. Owen Connelly, *French Revolution/Napoleonic Era* (New York: Holt, Rinehart and Winston, 1979), 169–72.

21. Connelly, *French Revolution*, 180–81.

22. Moorehead, *Dancing to the Precipice*, 235–37.

23. Lara Jennifer Moore, *Restoring Order: The Ecole des Chartes and the Organization of Archives and Libraries in France, 1820–1870* (Duluth, Minn.: Litwin Books, LLC, 2008), 242–45.

24. Adams, *Gouverneur Morris*, 250.

Bibliography

Adams, William Howard. *Gouverneur Morris: An Independent Life*. New Haven, Conn.: Yale University Press, 2003.

Alder, Ken. *The Measure of All Things: The Seven-Year Odyssey that Transformed the World*. London: Abacus, 2004.

Andress, David. *The Terror: The Merciless War for Freedom in Revolutionary France*. New York: Farrar, Straus and Giroux, 2005.

Aprile, Sylvie. *Le siècle des exiles: Bannis et proscrits de 1789 à la Commune*. Paris: CNRS Editions, 2010.

"Archives parlementaires de 1787 à 1860, recueil complet de débats législatifs et politiques des chambres françaises." *Première série (1787–1799)*. Ed. Jérôme Mavidal et al., 82 vols. Paris (1867–1913) 28: 326, 362.

Arnaud, Claude. *Chamfort: A Biography*. Trans. Deke Dusinberre. Chicago: University of Chicago Press, 1992.

Bailey, Colin. B. "Collectors of French Painting and the French Revolution." *1789: French Art During the Revolution* exhibition catalog, Los Angeles Museum of Art. Ed. Alan Wintermute. New York: Colnaghi, 1989.

———. "LeBrun et le commerce d'art pendant le Blocus continental." *Revue de l'Art 63* (1984): 35–47.

Baillio, Joseph. *Elisabeth Vigée-LeBrun, 1755–1842* exhibition catalog, Kimbell Art Museum. Fort Worth, Tex.: Kimbell Art Museum, 1982.

Balayé, Simone. *La Bibliothèque Nationale des Origines à 1800*. Geneva: Librairie Droz, 1988.

———. "La Bibliothèque Nationale pendant la Révolution." *Histoire des bibliothèques françaises: Les bibliothèques de la Révolution et du xix siècle, 1789–1914*. Vol. 3: 71–83. Ed. Dominique Varry. Paris: Promodis—Éditions du Cercle de la Librairie, 1988.

Belote, Theodore Thomas, ed. "The Scioto Speculation and the French Settlement of Gallipolis: A Study in Ohio Valley History." *University Studies*. Series II, Vol. 3, No. 3, September–October 1907: 5–82. Cincinnati, Ohio: University of Cincinnati Press.

———. "Selections from the Gallipolis Papers." *Quarterly Publication of the Historical and Philosophical Society of Ohio* II, no. 2, April–June 1907: 39–92. Cincinnati, Ohio: Press of Jennings and Graham.

Bienvenu, Richard T. *The Ninth of Thermidor: The Fall of Robespierre*. Oxford: Oxford University Press, 1968.

Blanc, Olivier. *Last Letters: Prisons and Prisoners of the French Revolution, 1793–1794*. Trans. Alan Sheridan. New York: Farrar, Straus and Giroux (Michael de Capua Books), 1987.

Brissot de Warville, Jacques-Pierre. *New Travels in the United States of America, 1788*. Trans. Mara Soceanu Vamos and Durand Echeverria. Cambridge, Mass.: Belknap Press of Harvard University Press, 1964.

Buchez, P.-J.-B., and P. C. Roux, eds. *Histoire parlementaire de la Révolution française depuis 1789 jusqu'à l'Empire*. Paris: Paulin, 1833–1838.

Buzot, François-Nicolas-Louis. *Mémoires de F.-N.-L. Buzot, Membre de l'Assemblée Constituante et député à la Convention Nationale par le département de L'Eure, Année 1793*. N. A. F. 1730. Paris: Bibliothèque Nationale, Dept. des Manuscrits.

Carpenter, Kristy, and Philip Mansel, eds. *The French Émigrés in Europe and the Struggle against Revolution, 1789–1814*. New York: St. Martin's Press, 1999.

Chamfort, Sébastien–Roch Nicolas. *Products of the Perfected Civilization: Selected Writings of Chamfort*. Trans. W. S. Merwin. San Francisco: North Point Press, 1984.

Childs, Francis S. *French Refugee Life in the United States: An American Chapter of the French Revolution*. Baltimore, Md.: Johns Hopkins Press, 1940.

Clarke, Joseph. *Commemorating the Dead in Revolutionary France: Revolution and Remembrance, 1789–1799*. Cambridge: Cambridge University Press, 2007.

Collection Deloynes. *Salon criticism (1783–1824)*. Paris: Bibliothèque Nationale, Cabinet des Estampes.

Collection Ginguené. *N. A. F. 9192, 9193, 9195*. Paris: Bibliothèque Nationale, Dept. des Manuscrits.

Connelly, Owen. *French Revolution/Napoleonic Era*. New York: Holt, Rinehart & Winston, 1979.

Correspondance 1793. Letters from Madame Roland to Buzot. N. A. F. 1730. Paris: Bibliothèque Nationale, Dept. des Manuscrits.

"Correspondance relative à l'administration et au personnel de la Bibliothèque royale II, 1781–1792." Archive 47. Paris: Bibliothèque Nationale, Dept. des Manuscrits.

Darnton, Robert. *George Washington's False Teeth: An Unconventional Guide to the Eighteenth Century*. New York: W. W. Norton, 2003.

Dauban, C. A., ed. *Mémoires Inédits de Pétion et Mémoires de Buzot & de Barbaroux, accompagnés de Notes Inédites de Buzot et de nombreux documents inédits sur Barbaroux, Buzot, Brissot, etc.* Paris: Henri Plon, 1866.

De Diesbach, Ghislain. *Histoire de l'Emigration, 1789–1814*. Revised edition. Paris: Librairie Académique Perrin, 1984.

De Ferrières, Marquis. *Correspondance inédité*. Paris: Armand Colin, 1932.

De la Tour du Pin, Mme. La Marquise. *Journal d'une Femme de Cinquante Ans, 1778–1815*. 2 vols. Paris, 1903, 1920.

Dépenses de la Bibliothèque nationale, 1791—An X, états et traitements. F17 3339. Paris: Archives Nationales.

Dossier Chamfort. F7 4638. Paris: Archives Nationales.

Echeverria, Durand. *Mirage in the West: A History of the French Image of American Society to 1815*. New York: Octagon Books, 1966.

Edmonds, W. D. *Jacobinism and the Revolt of Lyon, 1789–1793*. New York: Oxford University Press, 1990.

Eliel, Carol S. "Genre Painting During the Revolution and the Goût Hollandais." *1789: French Art During the Revolution* exhibition catalog, ed. by Alan Wintermute. New York: Colnaghi, 1989.

Ellery, Eloise. *Brissot de Warville: A Study in the History of the French Revolution*. Boston and New York: Houghton Mifflin, 1915; reprint New York: Burt Franklin, 1970.

Emile-Mâle, Gilberte. "Jean-Baptiste Piere LeBrun (1748–1813): Son Rôle Dans l'Histoire de la Restauration des Tableaux du Louvre." *Paris et Île-de-France 8*. Paris (1956): 371–417.

Evans, Sian. *The Memoirs of Elisabeth Vigée-LeBrun*. Bloomington: Indiana University Press, 1989.

Fitzsimmons, Michael P. *The Night the Old Régime Ended: August 4, 1789 and the French Revolution*. University Park: Pennsylvania State University Press, 2003.

Fritzsche, Peter. "Specters of History: On Nostalgia, Exile, and Modernity." *American Historical Review* 106, no. 5 (December 2001): 1587–1618.

———. *Stranded in the Present: Modern Time and the Melancholy of History*. Cambridge, Mass.: Harvard University Press, 2004.

Gallet, Michel. "La Maison de Mme. Vigée-LeBrun, rue du Gros Chênet." *Gazette des Beaux Arts* (November 1960): 275–84.

Gallipolis Papers, III: C, 33–67. Cincinnati Historial Society, Cincinnati, Ohio.

Gerhard, Anselm. *The Urbanization of Opera: Music Theater in Paris in the Nineteenth Century*. Trans. Mary Whittall. Chicago and London: University of Chicago Press, 1998.

Ginguené, Louis, ed. *Oeuvres de Chamfort*. 4 vols. Paris, 1795.

———. Preface to Chamfort's *Caractères et Anecdotes*. Paris: Crès, 1924.

Gould, Cecil. *Trophy of Conquest: The Musée Napoléon and the Creation of the Louvre*. London: Faber & Faber, 1965.

Greer, Donald. *The Incidence of Emigration During the French Revolution*. Cambridge, Mass.: Harvard University Press, 1951.

Hanson, Paul R. *The Jacobin Republic Under Fire: The Federalist Revolt in the French Revolution*. University Park: Pennsylvania State University Press, 2003.

Hardman, John. *Robespierre*. London: Longman, 1999.

Harris, Ann S., and Linda Nochlin. *Women Artists 1550–1950* exhibition catalog, Los Angeles Museum of Art. New York: Alfred A. Knopf, 1976.

Harsanyi, Doina. *Lessons from America: Liberal French Nobles in Exile, 1793–1798*. University Park: Pennsylvania State University Press, 2010.

Hérissay, Jacques. *Un Girondin: François Buzot, 1760–1794*. Paris: Perrin et Cie., Libraires-Éditeurs, 1907.

Hunt, Lynn. "The World We have Gained: The Future of the French Revolution." *American Historical Review* 108, no. 1 (February 2003): 1–19.

Johnson, James H. *Listening in Paris: A Cultural History*. Berkeley: University of California Press, 1995.

Jordan, David P. *The King's Trial: Louis XVI vs. the French Revolution*. Berkeley: University of California Press, 1979, 2004.

Knepper, George W. *Ohio and Its People*. Kent, Ohio: Kent State University Press, 1989.

Lawday, David. *Napoleon's Master: A Life of Prince Talleyrand*. New York: St. Martin's Press, 2007.

LeBrun, Jean-Baptiste Pierre. *Choix des tableaux les plus capitaux de la rare et précieuse collection recueillie dans L'Espagne et dans L'Italie, par M. LeBrun dans les années 1807 et 1808*. Paris, 1810.

———. *Galerie des peintres flamands, hollandaise et allemands*. 3 vols. Paris, 1792–1796. Paris: Bibliothèque Doucet, Fol. F212.

———. *Letters to the Minister of the Interior from LeBrun in 1792, 1793*. F17 1057, dossier 1, 1058, dossier 2, and 1059. Paris: Archives Nationales.

———. *Quelques Idées sur la Disposition, l'Arrangement et la Décoration du Muséum National*. Paris, 1794. Paris: Bibliothèque Doucet, 8 F990.

———. *Recueil de gravures au trait, à l'eau-forte et ombrées, d'après un choix de tableaux de toutes les écoles recueillis dans un voyage fait en Espagne, au midi de la France et en Italie dans les Années 1807 et 1808 par M. LeBrun, peintre, 2 tomes*. Paris: Imprimerie Didot jeune, 1809. Paris: Bibliothèque Doucet, 8 F1293.

———. *Réflexions sur le Muséum National*. Paris, 1792. Paris: Bibliothèque Doucet, 8 F1664.

Lefebvre, Georges. *The Coming of the French Revolution*. Trans. R. R. Palmer. Princeton, N.J.: Princeton University Press, 1947.

Letter dated 19 August 1792 from Interior Minister Roland to Sébastien Chamfort. T1458. Paris: Archives Nationales.

Louvet, Jean-Baptiste. *Mémoires de J.- B.Louvet, auteur de Faublas, membre de la Convention, etc.; de la Journée du 31 Mai suivis de Quelques Notices pour L'Histoire et le Récit de Mes Périls Depuis Cette Epoque Jusqu'à la Rentrée des Députés Proscrits dans L'Assemblée Nationale*. Paris: a la Librairie Historique, 1821.

———. *Mémoires de J.-B. Louvet, l'un des Représentans proscrits en 1793*. N. A. F. 1730. Paris: Bibliothèque Nationale, Dept. des Manuscrits.

Margerison, Kenneth. *Pamphlets and Public Opinion: The Campaign for a Union of Orders in the Early French Revolution*. West Lafayette, Ind.: Purdue University Press, 1998.

May, Gita. *Madame Roland and the Age of Revolution*. New York: Columbia University Press, 1970.

McClellan, Andrew. *Inventing the Louvre: Art, Politics, and the Origins of the Modern Museum in Eighteenth-Century Paris*. New York: Cambridge University Press, 1994.

Meadows, R. Darrell. "Engineering Exile: Social Networks and the French Atlantic Community, 1789–1809." *French Historical Studies* 23, no. 1 (Winter 2000): 67–102.

Moore, Lara Jennifer. *Restoring Order: The Ecole des Chartes and the Organization of Archives and Libraries in France, 1820–1870*. Duluth, Minn.: Litwin Books, 2008.

Moorehead, Caroline. *Dancing to the Precipice: Lucie de la Tour du Pin and the French Revolution*. London: Chatto & Windus, 2009.

Moreau-Zanelli, Jocelyne. *Gallipolis: Histoire d'un Mirage Américain au XVIII Siècle*. Paris: L'Harmattan, 2000.

Nicoullaud, Charles, ed. *Memoirs of the Countess de Boigne, 1781–1814*. New York: Charles Scribner's Sons, 1908.

Oliver, Bette W. *From Royal to National: The Louvre Museum and the Bibliothèque Nationale*. Lanham, Md.: Lexington Books, 2007.

———. *Orphans on the Earth: Girondin Fugitives from the Terror, 1793–1794*. Lanham, Md.: Lexington Books, 2009.

Papiers d'Eprémesnil. 158AP, carton 12. Paris: Archives Nationales.

Papiers Roland (1732–1793). N. A. F. 9532, 9533. Paris: Bibliothèque Nationale, Dept. des Manuscrits.

Papiers Tripier-LeFranc. Documents, correspondence, reports, and inventories about Elisabeth Vigée-LeBrun and her family. Paris: Bibliothèque Doucet.

Papiers de Van Praet. Paris: Bibliothèque Nationale, Dept. des Manuscrits.

Passez, Anne-Marie. *Adélaide Labille-Guiard, 1749–1803*. Paris: Arts et métiers graphiques, 1973.

Perroud, Cl., ed. *J.-P. Brissot, Correspondance et Papiers*. Paris: Librairie Alphonse Picard & Fils, 1911.

———. *J.-P Brissot, Mémoires 1754–1793*. Paris: Librairie Alphonse Picard & Fils, 1910.

———. *Lettres de Madame Roland, vol. 2 (1788–1793)*. Paris: Imprimerie Nationale, 1900–1902.

———. *Mémoires de Madame Roland*. Paris: Plon, 1905.

Pétion, Jérôme. *Mémoires de Jérôme Pétion*. N. A. F. 1730. Paris: Bibliothèque Nationale, Dept. des Manuscrits.

Phillips, Roderick. *Putting Asunder: A History of Divorce in Western Society*. Cambridge, Mass.: Cambridge University Press, 1988.

Rice, Danielle. "Women and the Visual Arts." *French Women and the Age of Enlightenment*. Ed. Samia I. Spencer. Bloomington: Indiana University Press, 1984.

Riouffe, Honoré. *Mémoires d'un Détenu, pour servir à l'histoire de la tyrannie de Robespierre, 2nd. ed., revue et augmentée*. Paris: De l'Imprimerie d'Anjubault, L'An III de la Republique Française.

Rivers, John. *Louvet: Revolutionist & Romance Writer*. London: Hurst and Blackett Ltd., Paternoster House, E. C., 1910.

Roberts, James. *The Counter-Revolution in France, 1787–1830*. New York: St. Martin's Press, 1990.

Roberts, J. M., and John Hardman, eds. *French Revolution Documents, vol. 2: 1792–5*. Oxford: Blackwell, 1973.

Roberts, Warren. "Gouverneur Morris and Thomas Jefferson: Two Americans in Paris in 1789." *Consortium on the Revolutionary Era, 1750–1850, Selected Papers 2008*: 31–40.

———. *Jacques-Louis David and Jean-Louis Prieur, Revolutionary Artists: The Public and the Populace, and Images of the French Revolution*. Albany: State University of New York Press, 2000.

———. *Jacques-Louis David, Revolutionary Artist*. Chapel Hill: University of North Carolina Press, 1989.

Roche, Daniel. *France in the Enlightenment*. Trans. Arthur Goldhammer. Cambridge, Mass./London: Harvard University Press, 1998.

Rolland-Michel, Marianne. *Anne Vallayer-Coster*. Paris: Comptoir international du livre, 1970.

Rosenberg, Pierre. Introduction to *French Painting 1774–1830: The Age of Revolution* exhibition catalog. Detroit, Mich.: Wayne State University, 1975.

Rosenfeld, Sophia. "AHR Forum on Being Heard: A Case for Paying Attention to the Historical Ear." *American Historical Review* 116, no. 2 (April 2011): 316–34.

Sanders, Alain. *Petit Chronique de la Grande Terreur*. Maule: Éditions de Présent, 1989.

Scarfe, Francis. *André Chénier: His Life and Work, 1762–1794*. Oxford: Clarendon Press, 1965.

Schama, Simon. *Citizens: A Chronicle of the French Revolution*. New York: Alfred A. Knopf, 1989.

Sewell, William H., Jr. *A Rhetoric of Bourgeois Revolution: The Abbé Sieyès and What is the Third Estate?* Durham, N. C.: Duke University Press, 1994.

Sheriff, Mary. *The Exceptional Woman: Elisabeth Vigée-LeBrun and the Cultural Politics of Art*. Chicago: University of Chicago Press, 1996.

Sydenham, M. J. *The Girondins*. London: University of London, Athlone Press, 1961.

Tackett, Timothy. *Becoming a Revolutionary: The Deputies of the French National Assembly and the Emergence of a Revolutionary Culture (1789–1790)*. Princeton, N.J.: Princeton University Press, 1996.

———. *When the King Took Flight*. Cambridge, Mass./London: Harvard University Press, 2003.

Traer, James F. *Marriage and the Family in Eighteenth-Century France*. Ithaca, N.Y.: Cornell University Press, 1980.

Troyat, Henri. *Catherine the Great*. New York: Berkeley Books, 1981.

Vente La Compagnie du Scioto. Minutier Central, Etudes V, XIII, XX. Paris: Archives Nationales.

Vigée-LeBrun, Elisabeth Louise. *Souvenirs*. 3 vols. Paris: Librairie de H. Fournier, 1835–1837.

Wells-Robertson, Sally. *Marguerite Gérard: 1761–1837*. Doctoral diss., New York University, 1978.

Whaley, Leigh. *Radicals: Politics and Republicanism in the French Revolution*. London: Sutton Publishing Ltd., 2000.

Index

Académie Royale de Peinture et de Sculpture, 20, 51, 52, 53

Alexandria, Virginia, 37–38

Amar, André, 74, 75, 90

American Revolution: aid from France, 6, 7; French fighters, 46; and French Revolution, 1, 6–7, 112; newspapers impact on the success of, 10

L'Ami du Peuple, 26, 42, 61

Ancien Régime: feudal rights during, 13; and new order, 1, 28; symbols of, 55; transition to constitutional monarchy, 7, 9, 10–11. *See also* monarchy

aristocrats: as members of the National Assembly, 13; purchase of lands in Ohio, 36–37. *See also* Compagnie des Vingt-Quatre ("the 24"); émigrés

artists. *See* LeBrun, Jean-Baptiste Pierre; Salons (painting); *specific artists*

d'Artois, Charles-Philippe (Comte), 19, 22, 23, 24, 104

Bailly, Jean-Sylvain: break with Estates General, 10; as mayor of Paris, 13, 97; as member of the Société de 1789, 56

Barbaroux, Charles, 81, 83, 86–87, 88, 100, 102

Barnave, Antoine, 8, 14

du Barry, Jeanne Bécu (Comtesse), 104

de Barth, Joseph, 39, 40

Bastille, 1, 3, 11–12, 13, 111

de Beaumetz, Bon Albert Brios, 46, 47

Bibliothèque Nationale. *See* National Library

Billaud-Varenne, Jean Nicolas, 74, 98

bookshops: in Philadelphia, 44, 45–46, 47; run by Louvet, 103; run by

Madame Brissot, 102

Bouquey, Thérèse, 81, 83, 84, 87, 88–89, 100

Bourbons: return to power, 45, 106, 107, 117; symbols of, 14; sympathy toward from Western rulers, 21

Brissot, Félicité, 73, 74, 77, 101–102

Brissot, Jacques-Pierre (de Warville): accounts in the *Patriote Français*, 15, 73, 113; appeal to the Committee of Public Safety, 74, 75–76; arrest, 71, 73; case referred to the National Convention, 71–72, 74, 101; defense, 72–74; description of United States, 6; execution, 77; in exile, 70–71; and family in the United States, 73; as Girondin leader, 26, 112; launching the *Patriote Français* newspaper, 10; memoir, 15, 70, 71, 74, 116; views on liberty, 77–78, 113; views on war, 26, 113; visit to the United States, 9–10, 73, 75, 113

Britain: and American colonies, 6; compared to France, 5, 6; recalling ambassador after Louis XVI's execution, 43

Brunswick Manifesto, 27

Buzot, François: as adversary of the Jacobins, 82, 116; biography, 82; as deputy in the National Assembly, 13; as deputy in the National Convention, 68, 82; as fugitive, 70, 81, 83, 86–87, 88, 89–90; as member in the National Convention, 25; memoir, 25, 70, 82; relationship with Manon Roland, 68, 69, 70

Capperonnier, Jean-Augustin, 63

Carra, Jean-Louis, 60, 61, 62–57

censorship, 9, 111–112

Chamfort, Sébastien-Roch Nicolas: arrest, 62; and Carra, 62; as co-director of the National Library, 60–61; and Committee of Public Safety, 61–62, 63; death, 63, 115; as director of the National Library, 61, 62; Ginguené as publisher, 63; as Girondin sympathizer, 60, 115; imprisonment, 62; as member of the Club of Thirty, 60; as member of the Société de 1789, 56; suicide attempt, 62; and Tobiésen-Duby, 61–62; views on Marat, 61, 115; as writer, 59–60, 62, 63

Charles X. *See* d'Artois, Charles-Philippe

Chénier, André: arrest, 58; execution, 59, 115; and Girondins, 58, 59; on the Jacobins, 56, 57–58, 59; political views, 56–59; relationship with David, 56, 57, 58, 115; writings, 56–58, 59, 63, 117

Chénier, Constantine, 59

Chénier, Marie-Joseph, 57–58, 59

Chénier, Sauveur, 58

Clavière, Etienne, 28

clergy: Civil Constitution of the Clergy, 24; as members of the First Estate, 7, 8, 9; and the revolutionary government, 67

Club of Thirty, 60

Commission des Monuments, 54

Commission Temporaire des Arts, 54

Committee of General Security, 74

Committee of Public Instruction, 55

Committee of Public Safety: Brissot appealing to, 74; and Chamfort, 61–62, 63; charging Manon Roland with conspiracy, 68, 69; David as member of, 56; establishment of, 43; members of arrested, 63–64; Robespierre as member of, 74, 90; sending troops to rebellious areas, 83

Compagnie des Vingt-Quatre ("the 24"): de Barth as leader of, 39, 40; and land purchase as émigrés, 35, 36, 39, 41, 42, 114; Lezay-Marnésia as leader of, 35, 39, 40

Conciergerie, 69, 71, 77, 95, 96, 97, 98

de Condé, Louis-Joseph de Bourbon (Prince), 26, 60

de Condorcet, Jean-Antoine-Nicolas de Caritat (Marquis): condemnation, 72; as member of the Club of Thirty, 60; as member of the Société de 1789, 56; sympathetic to Third Estate, 9

confiscations, 55–56, 60–61, 63

Constituent Assembly, 44, 45, 82, 89, 90

constitution: Brissot de Warville's views on, 10; Declaration of the Rights of Man and the Citizen as preface to, 14; and Louis XVI, 14, 24–26; suspended in 1793, 74; writing of by the National Assembly of France, 10–11

constitutional monarchy, 2, 7, 9, 10–11, 25–26

Constitution of the Year III (1795), 117

Coster, Jean Pierre Silvestre, 52

Council of Elders, 117

Council of Five Hundred, 103, 117

de Crèvecoeur, Hector St. John, 7

Danton, Georges Jacques: execution, 90; as Jacobin, 27; as leader of the Committee of Public Safety, 74; as minister of justice, 28, 42; in prison, 97

David, Jacques-Louis: arrest, 56, 63–64; as artist, 55, 56, 57, 64; and the Bourbon Restoration, 106, 107, 117; collaboration with LeBrun, 22, 30, 54, 56, 115; criticizing Jean Roland, 61; death, 107; as deputy in the National Convention, 54, 56, 59, 64, 115; in exile, 106, 107; as Napoleon's court painter, 64, 107, 115; political views, 56, 57–58, 64; relationship with André Chénier, 56, 57, 58, 115; as Robespierre's ally, 59, 63; and Vigée-LeBrun's work, 22

Declaration of Independence, 6

Declaration of the Rights of Man and the Citizen, 14

Desmoulins, Camille, 8, 11, 76, 97

Duchâstel, Gaspar Séverin, 81, 95, 96

Duer, William, 40
Dumouriez, Charles (General), 43, 72
Dupont, François, 73
Duport, Adrien, 9
d'Eglantine, Fabre, 98, 117
émigrés: after the fall of the monarchy, 42; colonies established by, 19–20; Compagnie des Vingt-Quatre ("the 24") as, 35, 36, 39–40, 41, 42, 114; first group, 37–41; and Indians, 39, 40; legislation regarding, 19, 26, 29; naturalization in the United States, 42; second group, 42; in United States, 2, 3, 35–48, 114–115

Enlightenment, 5, 63
d'Eprémesnil, M. Jean-Jacques (Duc), 36–37, 41
Estates General: Madame de la Tour du Pin views on, 45; meeting called by Louis XVI, 8–11; opening ceremony, 10
executions: of Brissot, 77; of Chénier, 59; of Duchâstel, 95; of Girey-Dupré, 97; of Girondins, 67, 77, 78, 81, 96–97, 116; of Louis XVI, 2, 43, 113; of Manon Roland, 67, 70, 97, 116; of Marie Antoinette, 67; of Robespierre, 91; of Roucher, 59; of Saint-Just, 91; of Sillery, 77; during the Terror, 4, 67, 75, 82, 91, 96, 98–99, 112
exhibitions. *See* Salons (painting)
exile: of Comte d'Artois, 19; of Comte de Provence, 19, 26, 52; physical and emotional toll, 111, 114; of Polignac family, 21, 22; during the Terror, 19–20; of Vigée-LeBrun, 3, 20–24, 28–29

de Ferrières-Marsay, Charles-Élie (Marquis), 9, 13, 16
festival honoring the Chateauvieux regiment, 57–58
Festival of National Unity, 55
feudal rights, abolished by the National Assembly, 13
Feuillants Club, 56
financial crisis (1788), 8

First Estate, 7, 9
Foulon, François, 12
France: compared to Britain, 5, 6; during the Enlightenment, 5; impact of American Revolution on, 6–7; population during the eighteenth century, 5, 7
Francis II, 26
Franklin, Benjamin, 6

Gallipolis, Ohio, 38, 39, 40–41, 42, 114
Garat, Dominique, 54, 55
Gérard, Marguerite: biography, 53–54, 107–108; compared to Vigée-LeBrun, 53–54, 108; exhibiting in LeBrun's gallery, 53; finances, 53, 107–108; painting style, 53, 107; as participant in Salons in Paris, 54, 107; portrait of Napoleon, 107
Gilbert du Motier, Marquis de Lafayette: as commander of the National Guard, 13, 15; fighting in the American Revolution, 7, 46; imprisonment, 42; as leader of the Patriot Party, 14; sympathetic to Third Estate, 9; political views, 56
Ginguené, Pierre-Louis, 60, 63
Girey-Dupré, Jean-Marie, 81, 97
Girondins: Amar's indictment against, 75; charged as traitors by the National Convention, 71–72; executions, 67, 77, 78, 81, 96–97, 116; expulsion from the National Convention, 2, 43–44, 61, 103, 112, 116; as fugitives, 81–82, 83, 84, 87–88, 90, 116; in the Legislative Assembly, 27; Louis XVI dismissing ministers, 27, 28; sentenced by the Revolutionary Tribunal, 69, 76; on the sentencing of Louis XVI, 43, 82; shift of general opinion on, 100–101, 102; as survivors of the Revolution, 103; trial of captured, 76–77; undermined by Robespierre, 42; widows of, 100, 101–102, 103. *See also specific individuals*
Gorsas, Antoine-Joseph, 81, 101
Gossec, François-Joseph, 57

Grétry, André: on the spectacle of the guillotine, 75
Guadet, Élie: as fugitive, 81, 83, 86, 87–88, 102; widow of, 100
Guion, Major, 37–38

Hamilton, Alexander, 40, 44
Hébert, Jacques, 27, 98
d'Herbois, Collot, 58, 74
Holland: recalling ambassador after Louis XVI's execution, 43

income of French population, eighteenth century, 7

Jacobin Club, 26, 56, 70, 74
Jacobins: in the aftermath of the Revolution, 117; André Chénier against, 56, 57–58, 59; Brissot as adversary of, 26, 97, 112; Buzot as adversary of, 82; favoring execution of Louis XVI, 43; Terror as an effort to preserve the Republic, 112. *See also specific individuals*
Jefferson, Thomas, 12
July Monarchy, 118

Labille-Guiard, Adélaide: accepted to the Académie Royale, 51; compared to Vigée-LeBrun, 51; ordered to destroy painting, 52; as participant in Salons in Paris, 51, 52; political views, 51–52
de Lafayette. *See* Gilbert du Motier, Marquis de Lafayette
de Launay, Bernard Rene Jourdan (Comte), 11–12
LeBrun, Charles, 54
LeBrun, Jean-Baptiste Pierre: arrest, 29; and art confiscations, 55–56; as art dealer, 20, 24, 30, 53, 56, 105–106, 115; collaboration with David, 22, 30, 54, 56, 115; death, 106; defending his wife, 28–29; discrediting the Museum Commission, 54, 61; divorcing his wife, 29–30, 104; as expert in Dutch painting, 30, 53, 55, 106; interest in contemporary artists, 53, 54; on Napoleon's

influence in art, 106; and the national museum, 3, 22, 30, 54–56, 115; relationship with Jean Roland, 54; sales of Spanish art, 106
Legislative Assembly: appointing a provisional executive council, 28; decree on émigrés, 26; dissensions with the Constituent Assembly, 112; factions within, 25, 26, 27, 28; LeBrun's request to, 28; and Louis XVI's powers, 24–26, 27; and social unrest in Paris, 27–28
Leopold II, 26
Lezay-Marnésia, Albert, 40, 41
Lezay-Marnésia, Claude-François (Marquis): encouraging emigration to Philadelphia, 40; land purchase, 37; return to France, 41; on superiority of Indians, 40
Liberal Empire, 118
Lodoiska (wife of Louvet), 84, 85, 86, 103
Louis XVI: and constitutional monarchy, 2, 10–11, 25–26; and the constitution of 1791, 14, 24–26; dismissing ministers, 11, 28; establishing the National Guard, 13; execution, 2, 43, 113; financial support to United States, 8; flight to Varennes, 19, 25, 71; Girondins on the sentencing of, 43, 82; leaving Versailles, 15; and the Legislative Assembly, 24–26, 27; Liancourt's support to, 47; and March of Women, 14–15; meeting of the Estates General, 8–11; portrait by David, 57; reaction to new government, 11, 14; removal from power, 27–28, 72; vetos, 26, 27; war declaration against Austria, 26
Louis XVIII. *See* de Provence (Comte)
Louvet, Jean-Baptiste: account of social unrest of 1789, 12; in the aftermath of the Revolution, 100, 102–103; bookshop, 103; death, 103; as described by Manon Roland, 83; education, 83–84; as fugitive, 81, 83, 84–86; as Girondin, 12, 84, 100, 102, 103; literary career, 12, 84; as

member of the National Convention, 12, 84, 85, 86, 100, 102, 103; memoir, 12, 86, 103; political views, 84; as publisher of Manon Roland memoir, 103; and wife, 84, 85, 86, 103
Louvre, 30, 52, 54–56. *See also* Napoleon Museum; National Museum

Marat, Jean-Paul: assassination, 61, 74, 115; as candidate of the Paris Commune, 42; as editor of *L'Ami du Peuple*, 26, 42, 61; views on war, 26
Marchena, Don José, 71, 73, 81, 95
March of the Women, 14–15
Marie Antoinette: colony in Ohio named in honor of, 39; execution, 67; hope for the restoration of the monarchy, 26; leaving Versailles, 15, 25; Vallayer-Coster sponsored by, 52; and Vigée-LeBrun, 20, 22, 52, 105
Marietta, Ohio, 39–40
memoirs: of Brissot, 15, 70, 71, 74, 116; of Buzot, 25, 70, 82; of Girondin fugitives, 81, 83, 88–89; of Louvet, 12, 86, 103; of Madame de la Tour du Pin, 45, 115; of Manon Roland, 28, 68–69, 103; of Riouffe, 95–100, 116; of Vigée-LeBrun, 20, 21, 23, 29, 30, 54, 104, 105, 106, 114
Méricourt, Théroigne de, 58
Mirabeau, Honoré Gabriel Riqueti (Comte), 10, 43, 56
monarchy: fall of, 3, 27–28, 42, 47, 111; July Monarchy, 118; power of, eroded, 14; transition to constitutional, 7, 9, 10–11
Moreau de Saint-Méry, Méderic-Louis-Elie, 44, 45–46, 48
Mounier, Jean-Joseph, 14
Musée Napoleon. *See* Napoleon Museum
Museum Commission, 54, 61

Napoleon Bonaparte: Civil Code (1804), 107; David as court painter of, 64, 107, 115; influence in art, 106; and the outcomes of the Continental blockade, 106; portrait by Gérard, 107; reign, 105, 117, 118; Vigée-LeBrun on, 104
Napoleon Museum, 56
National Assembly: abolishing feudal rights, 13; adoption of the Civil Constitution of the Clergy, 24; adoption of the Declaration of the Rights of Man and the Citizen, 14; and constitution writing, 10–11; establishment of, 10; members of escorting the royal family to Paris, 15; reforms, 24
National Convention: and Brissot's case, 71–72, 74, 101; Buzot as deputy, 68, 82; charging Girondins as traitors, 72; Council of Five Hundred as legislative successor, 103; David as deputy, 54, 56, 59, 64, 115; decision to execute Louis XVI, 43; dissolution, 101; elections, 28, 42; establishment of the Revolutionary Calendar, 67; expulsion of Girondins from, 2, 43–44, 61, 103, 112, 116; factional divisions within, 42–43, 45, 56, 61, 82, 84, 89, 103, 112; Jean Roland's speech to, 42; Louvet as member, 12, 84, 85, 86, 100, 102, 103; against Robespierre, 90–91; suspending the constitution of 1793, 74; and the Terror, 74, 91; during the Thermidorian Reaction, 116–117
National Guard, 13, 15, 91
National Library: Capperonnier as director, 63; Carra as co-director, 60; Chamfort as co-director/director, 60–61, 62; Jean Roland and protection of collections, 60–61; Villebrune as director, 63
National Museum: collections, 55–56; LeBrun and, 3, 22, 30, 54–56, 115; as national symbol, 55. *See also* Louvre; Napoleon Museum
National Theater, 62
Necker, Jacques, 11, 13, 104, 112
New York, 45
de Noailles, Louis-Marie (Vicomte), 7, 46

Ohio: émigrés settling in, 35–41, 42, 114; land purchase by "the 24," 35, 36, 39, 41, 42; land sales by Compagnie du Scioto, 35–37; Major Guion escorting émigrés to, 37–38
d'Orléans, Louis Philippe (Duc), 24

Paris: in 1780, 5; in 1797, 117; before the elections, 82; social unrest, 11–12, 27–28
Paris Commune, 27–28, 42, 58, 76, 91, 111, 113, 118
Patriote Français, 10, 15, 73, 76, 97, 113
Patriot Party, 14
Penn, William, 6
Pétion, Jérôme: as fugitive, 81, 83, 86–87, 88, 89–90, 101, 102; as mayor of Paris, 43–44, 116
Philadelphia: Beaumetz as émigré in, 46, 47; bookshops, 44, 45–46, 47; as destination for émigrés, 2, 37, 39, 40, 44, 45, 46, 72, 73; Liancourt as émigré in, 47; Saint-Méry as émigré in, 44, 45–46, 48
Picault, Jean Michel, 54
Playfair, William, 36, 40
Polignac family, as émigrés, 21, 22
de Provence (Comte), 19, 26, 52

Ramel de Nogaret, Dominique-Vincent, 107
republic: *versus* constitutional monarchy, 25; Festival of National Unity, 55; Jacobins' efforts to preserve from the Girondins, 112
Revolutionary Calendar, 67
Revolutionary Tribunal, 69–70, 75, 76
Riouffe, Honoré: account on Manon Roland in prison, 96–97; under arrest, 81, 95–96; memoir of time in prison, 95–100, 116
Robespierre, Augustin de, 91
Robespierre, Maximilien de: blamed for the September massacres, 42; calling for a "Government of Terror," 74; as candidate of the Paris Commune, 42, 113; David as ally, 59, 63; and Desmoulins, 97; execution, 91; fall of, 2, 86, 90–91; as

Jacobin leader, 26, 27, 74; as member of the Rolands' circle, 90; portrait by Labille-Guiard, 52; *versus* Tallien at the National Convention, 87, 90–91; undermining the Girondins, 42, 43; on war, 26, 113
la Rochefoucauld-Liancourt, François Alexandre Frédéric (Duc), 46, 47, 56
Roederer, Pierre-Louis, 56
Roland, Jean: accusations against, 43; criticisms about, 54, 61; dismissed by Louis XVI, 28; and the Girondins, 43, 60, 61; in hiding, 61, 68; Louvet working for, 84; as minister of the interior, 27, 42, 60, 61; and protection of art works and library materials, 60–61; resignation, 61; speech to the National Convention, 42; suicide, 70
Roland, Manon: arrest, 61, 68; charged with conspiracy against the revolution, 68, 69–70; description of by Riouffe, 96–97; description of Louvet, 83; execution, 67, 70, 97, 116; imprisonment, 68–69, 96–97; memoir, 28, 68–69, 103; relationship with Buzot, 68, 69, 70; on Robespierre, 42, 90
Roucher, Jean-Antoine, 59, 117
Rousseau, Jean Jacques, 6, 7

Saint-Just, Louis-Antoine: accusations against Brissot, 71–72, 75; accusations against Buzot, 82; arrest and execution, 91
Salle, Jean Baptiste, 81, 83, 86, 87–88, 102
Salons (painting): Gérard and, 54, 107; Labille-Guiard and, 51, 52; Vigée-LeBrun and, 20, 22, 23, 29, 51, 105
Santerre, Antoine Joseph, 27, 28
Scioto Co.: perceived as unreliable, 37, 39, 40, 42; *Prospectus*, 35–36, 39, 114; land sales by, 35–37; reimbursing émigrés, 38; supplies to émigrés, 38–39
Second Empire, 118
Second Estate, 7
September massacres, 42, 89, 97

Servan, Joseph, 28
Sieyès, Abbé: attending Chamfort's funeral, 63; break with Estates General, 10; as leader of the Patriot Party, 14; on the Third Estate, 8, 9, 60
Sillery, Charles Alexander, 77
social unrest: March of Women, 14–15; in Paris, 11–12, 27–28
Société de 1789, 56, 60
Souque, Joseph, 70–71, 73, 99, 100
de Staël, Germaine (Madame), 104

Talleyrand, Charles-Maurice de: exile to the United States, 44–45, 47–48, 115; friendship with Hamilton, 44; as member of the Club of Thirty, 60; as member of the First Estate, 9, 44; return to France, 44
Tallien, Jean-Lambert, 47, 58, 83, 87, 90–91
Talon, Omer Antoine, 46–47
Tennis Court Oath, 10
Terror: censorship during 1793–1794, 111; executions during, 4, 67, 75, 82, 91, 96, 98–99, 112; Ginguené on, 63; Grétry on the spectacle of the guillotine, 75; as a Jacobin effort to preserve the Republic, 112; and the National Convention, 74, 91; Revolutionary Tribunal as instrument of, 75; Robespierre calling for a "Government of Terror," 74. *See also* émigrés
Thermidorian Reaction (1794–1795), 116–117
Third Estate: Liancourt as member, 47; at meeting of the Estates General, 8–9, 10; members of, 7, 9, 10, 78
Third Republic, 118
Tobiésen-Duby, Pierre-Ancher, 61–62
de la Tour du Pin, Jean-Frédéric (Marquis), 45, 47
de la Tour du Pin, Lucy, 44, 45, 47, 115
Treaty of Paris (1763), 6
tricolor, as symbol of the Revolution, 13
Troquart, Baptiste, 87, 88, 102–103

Trudaine de Montigny, Charles-Louis, 56
Trudaine de Sablière, Charles-Michel, 56

United States: Congress, 40–41; and émigrés from France, 2, 3, 20, 35–48, 114–115; exchanges with France, 6–7; financial support from Louis XVI, 8; naturalization of émigrés, 42; reform impact on France, 6–7; and social values, 112, 113

Vadier, Marc, 74, 90
Valady, J. G. C. S. J. J. Yzarn (Marquis), 81, 83
Vallayer-Coster, Anne: biography, 52–53; exhibiting at the Paris Salons, 53; as member of Académie Royale de Peinture et de Sculpture, 53; sponsored by Marie Antoinette, 52
de Vaudreuil, Joseph Hyacinthe Francois de Paule de Rigaud (Comte), 22–23, 60, 104
Versailles, 14, 15
Vigée, Etienne, 29, 30–31
Vigée-LeBrun, Elisabeth: compared to Gérard, 53–54, 108; compared to Labille-Guiard, 51; death, 105; in exile, 3, 20–24, 28–29, 51; and husband, 20, 28–30, 54, 104, 106, 115; life after the Revolution, 103–105; as member of the Académie Royale de Peinture et de Sculpture, 20, 53; as member of the Roman Academia di San Luca, 21; memoir, 20, 21, 23, 29, 30, 54, 104, 105, 106, 114; on Napoleon, 104; portraits painted by, 20, 22, 23, 104–105; as participant in Salons in Paris, 20, 22, 23, 29, 105; relationship with Comte de Vaudreuil, 22–23; return from exile, 24, 30, 103–104
Vigée, Louis, 53
de Villebrune, Jean-Baptiste Lefebvre, 63
Vivant-Denon, Dominique, 105
Voltaire (François-Marie Arouet), 6

Washington, George, 37

widows of Girondins, 100, 101–102, 103

women artists. *See* Gérard, Marguerite; Labille-Guiard, Adélaide; Vallayer-Coster, Anne; Vigée-LeBrun, Elisabeth

writers: in France on American colonies, 6–7; *See also specific writers*

About the Author

Bette W. Oliver of Austin, Texas, is an independent scholar with a PhD in modern European history from the University of Texas at Austin. A specialist in late eighteenth-century France, she is the author of *From Royal to National: The Louvre Museum and the Bibliothèque Nationale* (2007) and *Orphans on the Earth: Girondin Fugitives from the Terror, 1793-1794* (2009). With an educational and professional background in both journalism and history, she served as the associate editor of the interdisciplinary journal *Libraries & Culture*, published by the University of Texas Press, from 1986 to 2005, and she continues to work as an editorial consultant. In addition, she is the author of ten volumes of poetry, much of it about France.